PSYCHOLOGY *of* BUREAUCRATS

PSYCHOLOGY
of
BUREAUCRATS

Dr PK Agrawal, IAS
(Former Additional Chief Secretary, West Bengal)
Parvez Dewan, IAS
(Former Secretary, Govt of India)

Manas Publications
(We Convert Fighters into Writers)
New Delhi - 110 002 (INDIA)

MANAS PUBLICATIONS
(We Convert Fighters into Writers)
(Publishers, Library Suppliers, Importers & Exporters)
4402/5-A, Ansari Road (Opp. HDFC Bank)
Darya Ganj, New Delhi - 110 002 (India)
Phones: Off.: 011-23260783, 23265523, Res.: 011-23842660
E-mail: manaspublications@gmail.com
manaspublications@yahoo.com
Website: www.manaspublications.in

ISBN 978-81-7049-496-6
₹ 595.00

Designed at
Manas Publications

Printed in India at
R.K. Print Service, Delhi
and published by Mrs Suman Lata for
Manas Publications, 4402/5-A,
Ansari Road (Opp HDFC Bank),
Darya Ganj, New Delhi - 110002 (INDIA)

To

those unrecognized

Bureaucrats

who

worked sincerely and honestly

for the

Country

Contents

Preface

The bureaucrats impact the society in a big way as they are the main constituent of what is called government. Howsoever the private sector may expand, they also look at the bureaucrats for policy planning, macro-economy and maintenance of law and order. Therefore, it is very important for everybody to know how bureaucrats will behave or react when they approach them for some work. His behaviour can only be inferred after the study of his mind or ego which is called psychology.

A bureaucrat is a highly egoist person. The ego can be assessed from one's outer personality, his environment, experience and will-power. A bureaucrat is a part of the society. When a person joins the government, he or she brings along experience of his/her past. If a person comes from the lower middle class, he will be close to the stake-holders. A middle class bureaucrat knows his origin but tries to be in the upper class. Officers, who come from the middle class form bulk of the bureaucracy. They are the most vocal and represent the bureaucracy. Upper class bureaucrats maintain their class identity and are self-oriented, career-minded from the beginning. They don't have much commitment to the job or to the mission of the organization. The economic characteristics of the Indian bureaucracy are those of the middle class. The pay, perks or status one gets in the bureaucracy except Class IV or 'D' Group employees make one to belong to the middle class.

The personality of the bureaucrat is like the form of an iceberg whose ninth tenth part is hidden. The bureaucrat is apt in the art of hiding his real personality. His decisions, reaction and even mood have an impact on the well-being of society. He is an intelligent person who has the capacity to read the pulse of his stake-holders, mainly the public, and to respond suitably. In developing and less-developed countries, bureaucrats are the cream of society. Even in developed countries bureaucrats are socially well-recognized. Therefore, many young people in spite of high salaries in the private sector prefer to join government or semi-government organizations. These people, however, develop negativities after joining the government because they have so many clients to oblige who have competitive demands and sometimes even rival demands. Therefore, the brain of such a bureaucrat is a poor receptor of outside inputs, reflexes or light. As the whole society is his work field, he keeps his nose sensitive to smell rumours.

In developing and less-developed countries bureaucrats call the shot in the polity. They are the final referees or umpires of the game of administration or public service or public management. They are the winners. Yet they are part of Weber's organization which is indifferent, formal and continuous one.

It is as group so powerful that one bureaucrat finds himself as helpless before it and compromises at each stage. He has to manage his ego. An inflated ego often comes into conflict with other persons. In order to justify the volume of his ego, he has to claim credit for achievements which may be result of hard work done by other people and not by himself. At the same time, he has to deny responsibilities for a failed action. The right size ego works in bureaucracy which can be achieved by adopting right attitude in life.

This book helps to read the psychology of differently placed bureaucrats and also how the performance of bureaucrats can be measured and improved to achieve the mission of the bureaucratic organization and society in general.

The first chapter of the book dwells on the fact that a government official has a rigid ego because he has security of job and power to impact others. He has no defined boss as public is the ultimate boss. Even in socialist countries like erstwhile USSR and China, the bureaucracy is an unnecessary evil. A government is said to be successful if it rides on the horse called bureaucracy. There is no point to criticize or despise the bureaucrats. The experts on bureaucratic functioning find Netherlands as the best bureaucracy followed by Finland because these countries have decentralized system of bureaucracy. The decentralized bureaucracy also exists in United States, Soviet Russia and China, India, Canada, Australia and Germany. United Kingdom and France have over-centralized bureaucracy. The Middle-East countries and small African and Latin American countries have bureaucracy community of feudal lords who rule those countries. Other countries have the bureaucratic set-up in between. The self-image of an Indian bureaucrat, French bureaucrat, socialist bureaucrat and bureaucrats of other Asian countries, African and Latin American countries and of US bureaucrats have been sketched to cover global scene of practical psychology. The conclusion is arrived at that the emotional component is sometimes more important than the rational component. A bureaucrat can be more efficient if he understands the psychological process by which the bureaucrats operate.

In the second chapter, the behavioural pattern of bureaucrats in India has been analysed in various governments at the Centre, States of Uttar Pradesh, Bihar, Jharkhand, West Bengal, Odisha, Andhra Pradesh, Tamil Nadu, Kerala, Karnataka, Goa, Maharashtra, Gujarat, Rajasthan, Punjab, Haryana, Jammu and Kashmir, Madhya Pradesh, Chhattisgarh, Uttarakhand, Delhi and other Union Territories. The bureaucrats of Gujarat have been rated as ideal ones whereas Tamil Nadu bureaucrats have been found to possess requisite work culture. The Andhra Pradesh bureaucrats are forward-looking whereas bureaucrats in Rajasthan and Punjab are feudal and aristocrat respectively. On the other hand, bureaucrats in Assam are traditional and whereas in Kerala and West Bengal are rule-bound bureaucrats. This gives the whole parameter of working of bureaucrats which reflect their applied psychology at work.

Chapter three contains the institution of Ombudsman prevalent in various countries to prevent misuse of bureaucratic authority. There are now six types of Ombudsman at all levels of government. The Ombudsman is very well-established position in Sweden, Finland and Norway. Other countries are fast following it to satisfy public outcry against the misuse of power by bureaucracy. In India, even the government at the Centre was changed because it failed to pass the Lokpal Act as suggested by the agitationists led by social activist Anna Hazare in the year 2013. It is now different story that even the incoming government has not enforced the Act of 2013 which was passed in frustration by the outgoing government before they lost at the hustings. The scenario of appointment of Ombudsman i e Lokayuktas in various States of India has also been brought out. In the end, it is suggested that the introduction on codification of the administrative law in India can cure all ills being faced by the bureaucrats as well as public because it will be the code of working for the bureaucrats as well as code of professional ethics for them.

In the fourth chapter, values of the American bureaucrats have been highlighted to showcase that intrinsic values of bureaucracy form his psychology. The bureaucrats in America have historically contributed to the efficiency and effectiveness to the entire process of governance and have competed with the private sector in US. Therefore, they are more output-oriented and less of rule-bound. They believe bureaucracy to toe line of the political party in power but the mood in US bureaucracy is changing after its members couldn't protect the bureaucrats in their actions in cases of Enron's failure, Watergate scandal, failure of CIA in Iraq and Clinton-Monica Lewinsky Affair, whereas the role of the bureaucracy in US has been appreciated in case of terrorist attack on the World Trade Towers and aftermath. Thus the trend in US is now from the 'spoils system' to the neutral and non-partisan public service. Of course, in US, the public servants always work in close co-operation with the private sector which is much more pervading and economically robust.

Chapter five deals with the need for motivation among bureaucrats and tools which can motivate a public servant and keep him in good working condition later on. A formula has also been devised which has taken into consideration the factors of motivation *viz* Macro Environment (weightage 12%), Financial Incentives (25%), Personnel Management (25%), Job Enrichment (13%) and Leadership (25%). The weightage factors may differ slightly from country to country and from time to time. However, significance to each factor will be based on subjective assessment. Thus, the chapter elaborates how such a personal or psychological factor like motivation of bureaucrat can be mathematically evaluated which will help to measure or ensure his efficiency at his work place.

In the sixth chapter, fear psychosis among bureaucrats has been highlighted. A bureaucrat has to function within conflicting claims and counter-claims. Therefore, sometimes he is not welcome at his work place. This creates psychological barriers in his job and insecurity of his job looms large in his mind creating mental and physical disorders. As a result, he suffers from various ailments. The traditional bureaucrats find it difficult to learn innovations very fast. This creates psychological problems in their personal life and is reflected in their working. As far as it can be lessened, it is better for the governmental system.

Seventh chapter demonstrates outward personality of a bureaucrat which is the reflection of his inner personality. It analyzes his inner conflicts which are not appreciated by his boss or society. However, Yoga as therapy can help him to overcome his ailments. It is laid down that psychological satisfaction is even more important than money.

Corruption among bureaucrats, has become a great problem worldwide. Positive psychology can help to tackle the corruption. Chapter eight holds that in cases of determined corrupt officials and political executives, independent judiciary and speedy prosecutional institutions are only safety valves. Corruption in the Indian polity has been projected as a case study.

Chapter nine deals ethics of bureaucrats which can cure all ills of bureaucrats. For that purpose, there should be a code of conduct of statutory guidelines to enforce objectivity, accountability, openness and integrity among bureaucrats. A code of conduct will guide a bureaucrat like friend, philosopher and guide. It will solve many of his problems. He will then be able to contribute more to the government and the society.

Tenth chapter dwells on psychology of bureaucrats in three different economic classes of the society.

Last chapter by Mr Parvez Dewan reveals his experience to deal with employees of private sector who are now being classified as a slightly different type of bureaucrats having similar psychology.

Thus, I have attempted to bring out various facets of psychology of bureaucrats all over the world. It is only through their cultural values, varied types of working and different traits of personalities, a person can gauge their psychology. As the bureaucrat is a public figure, his applied psychology in public arena has been focused. I am sure that this work will be welcome by all because the functioning of bureaucrats in governments directly impact the well-being of the society.

I thank my colleague in IAS Mr Parvez Dewan for his contribution on psychology of employees in the private sector.

Dr PK Agrawal

1

Psychology of Bureaucrats: An International Scenario

Psychology is the study of the mind and how it works. It encompasses the mental characteristics of a person or a group of persons like bureaucrats. The awareness of self is through the ego which defines one's personality. Behind personality is the hidden psychology which is dynamic. It depends mainly on three factors ie one's environment, experience and will-power. These three factors are always in flux. Ego depends on his present circumstances and past experiences. The environment of an individual is affected by numerous factors, one of them being one's location as measured on the scales of time and space which is always in flux. Second is the role of experience. The experiences of an individual are contained in a metaphorical memory box, which consists of images of past happenings, actions performed and the results thereof. The third and the most important factor that affects the ego is will-power. The thought force, which operates through the mind, has a wonderful quality of controlling itself. In view of this quality, individual ego ie a person can be what he or she decides to be. Thus, it is essential to know the psychology of a bureaucrat to study his attitude and behaviour.

A bureaucrat is government official who has a strong ego because he has security of job and power to impact others. He is concerned more with writing than the decision-making. But in a developing country like India, bureaucrat is the main decision-maker. Most of the decisions effecting people's lives emanate from his pen because in a democratic set-up like India, political executives come and go but this unelected person or selected person stays on and on until he retires. He is indifferent and impartial in his working and is bound by the constitution of the country which is the basic norms for his working. Therefore, he is responsible and is symbol of performance in government. He is thus, a pivot in the society around which many significant things happen.

He is thus a very important person about whom a person in society is interested to know as to how he eats, how he lives, how he works and how he thinks so that people can premeditate his decision and can act to make his decision favourable to them. He talks less but works or writes more. He is basically a thinker in the government. Thus, study of psychology of bureaucrats will help to plan how the things in future will shape in a polity and how the welfare of people can be ensured.

The class of bureaucrats starts from the peon to the Cabinet Secretary in the Union or Central Government. It includes police force except defence and paramilitary forces because the latter category has very few contact points with the citizens or civilians. Thus, study of psychology of bureaucrats is a complicated one and it encompasses a variety of categories of personnel who constitute wide variety of jobs performed from an employee in a Gram Panchayat or municipal body or local council or commune to the top official in the Central Government and from a peon in the office to the Secretary in a department or ministry. The working of a collective body specially the public elected one is at variance with the working of purely a bureaucratic organization that can be run on well-formulated rules and procedures without much intervention or inputs from the top. While working in different types of organizations, the people form different psychology due to habitual working and way of life.

However, the bureaucratic organization has been accepted as an unnecessary evil throughout the world in all times. The political masters who tried to overlook its significance went into oblivion and were dethroned by their own electorate like in the erstwhile Soviet Russia (USSR) and its allied countries in the Eastern Europe. The socialist junta themselves became bureaucrats.

Max Weber known as father of bureaucracy defined the 'bureaucracy' and thereby bureaucrat. His main emphasis is on formalism, hierarchy and rules which govern a bureaucrat.

Jennings presents a psycho-analytic theory of the bureaucrat as an 'anal erotic' type who seeks security by controlling his environment by regulations and procedures. Any number of psychological theories or mechanisms can be advanced, and a number of cultural interpretations are possible, eg by going back to the ancient Chinese Civil Service or by noting the development of bureaucracy in scientific societies, in universities, and in labour organizations in which reverence of traditions and customs is paramount, will probably help the growth of bureaucrats, whether the reverence be for religious, military, political, or philosophic traditions. Perhaps the Samurai of Japan, the priests of ancient Egypt, the Leninists of Russia, and the socialists of modern States have in bureaucratic terms more in common than they realize.[1]

> "The bureaucrat is the methodical man who has intent maintaining and perfecting the system.... He pours his aspirations into narrowly prescribed channelling of his efforts.... This need to put oneself in a bounded, limited role or activity is crucial to the act of accepting the life of an expert. Strong deposits in the personality feed this 'putting-in' complex."[2]

Parkinson, the doyen of humour on bureaucrats feels that bureaucrats are custodial type persons.

> "The custodial person will fear change and resent new ideas. Part of his reaction will be caused by inertia, indolence, ignorance, timidity, lack of imagination, feelings of inferiority, or fear of failure. But there are many things to be said in favour of instinctive fears of change and blind resentment against new ideas."[3]

The efficiency of the custodial person is based on predictability. The manager, or leader, or the clerk can be efficient only to the extent that he can predict what will happen.

> "Robert K Merton is the first to use the term pathology in connection with bureaucracy. Among the pathological symptoms that have been mentioned are 'trained incapacity' (Veblew); 'occupation psychosis' (Dewey); 'professional deformation' (Warnotte); 'displacement of goals', 'formalism', 'ritualism', 'rules become symbolic instead of utilitarian', 'non-logical pride of craft', 'personalization', 'arrogance', 'haughtiness' and 'vested interest' (Merton)."[4]

According to Srivastava (1976), Datta (1971), and Singh and Das (1971),

> "The bureaucratic culture inhibits normal development of human personality. The structure is inadequate in inducing commitment to work. Therefore, in such organizations, there are unreasonable demands for economic benefits."[5]
>
> "Motivation or commitment cannot come only from ideology. Correspondingly, structure and system of organization should also be attended to."[6]

There is no point to criticise or hate the bureaucrat. More the criticism of bureaucrat, more he becomes sullen and complacent. He is a part of the society. Therefore, many of his inner problems like adverse psychological behaviour has to be traced back in the environment he comes from or he lives in. The senior bureaucrats have a problem to control 93% members of bureaucracy who are Class III personnel ie clerks and Class IV employees ie peons. They constitute a solid vote bank of political parties. Accordingly, political executives look for them and they work for their support. This is specially a problem in the Indian bureaucracy. It is now becoming a problem for other countries:

> "Politicians, are none too popular at the present time. Perhaps the most extraordinary features of the present age is the contrast between our technical progress and our political stagnation. There are no new ideas seemingly in politics and the practice so far from progressing is obviously slipping back so that the word 'stagnation' is an under-statement. Our problem at the moment seems to be not one of progress but one of survival."[7]

Thus, experts like Parkinson even estimate a challenge for bureaucracy to survive. According to him, Netherlands has the best bureaucracy followed by Finland. The subdivided countries are the United States, Soviet Russia, China, India, Canada, Australia, Germany and the Netherlands. The two countries which are over-centralized are probably United Kingdom and France. Of course, countries in the Middle-East are over-centralized having feudal kings or monarch. So this type of bureaucracy exists in small African and Latin American countries where democracy is in name but actually community of feudal lords rule those countries. The situation in South Asian countries is in between the same. Let us now survey how the psychology of bureaucrats differ from country to country starting from India.

Indian Bureaucrats

He has a self-image of self-assurance, subordination and fear of termination of the job. His projected image is higher in society. Thus there is pseudoism in him that breeds psychological disorders. The Indian manager is more concerned with happiness, contentment and peace for himself and his near and dear. He wants to project himself as 'good man' and aims to self-actualization. His idealism in the practical situations, gives way to pragmatism.

His projected image is one of a person who is very busy in work. The work eats away all his vitals in life. The political system lets loose all the hell on him and mars his *bona fide* intentions too. He is sandwiched between his bureaucratic obligations and political pressures. This creates psychological imbalance in him. He looks sullen, bossy, supercilious and disorganized. He often fails to consider reactions or needs of others. He adopts a ready-made image in media. He poses himself as thorough in work and feels that he should look also thorough and overbearing. The High Courts and the Supreme Court are just there to harass him by calling him for contempt of Court though he alone is not to be blamed for his action. He himself looks scrubby and indicates through positive and body language that he cannot be bothered to talk to public. He is educated and is repository of all information and correct decision-making in the concerned seat or department or the ministry.

However, his received image is at odds with his projected image. He is a person in power but he hardly makes sincere efforts to exercise his power to deliver goods and services to the public who are his clients or customers in general. But his take home image is poor. However, he is still respected in the society because another window of the political executives is out of reach for the common public.

> "The visual image impact predominates, says Davies, quoting the finding of a professional psychologist, to the effect that 55% of the impression you make depends on what people see (your positive, facial expression, dress, body language etc), 38% on what they hear (the tone and pitch of your voice, clarity of speech etc); and only 7% on actual words you utter which in any case could have been written for you by someone else."[7]

The Indian Administrative Service is an unique instrument of governance peculiar and nothing[8] like it is found anywhere else in the world. This premium service is one which the people bank upon in spite of all turmoil, strife, political upheavals, foreign invasion and natural calamities. The IAS is a generalist service par excellence. However, due to political power on IAS, some cracks have been visible. Loyalties in the country kept shifting and officers gradually began to be identified with different political parties, factions, or individuals. For some State cadre officers, seeking the political umbrella became at first a convenient choice and for a smaller number, a necessity. Honesty and morality had become attributes of the past.

> "The service cannot be divorced from the society of which it is a segment. Over the years there has been a general decline in the moral and ethical standards of the society which is also reflected in the whole bureaucracy and could also be identified as a cause of deterioration of the IAS. Government servants have respect for rules and procedures in their self-interest and have disregard for their duties and responsibilities. The elite service has no faith in anti-poverty and asset-distribution programmes. However, they still feel that they are intellectually of high calibre, committed to the organization, action and result-focused, rational and logical, conscientious and risk takers, innovative and creative."[9]

However, the Indian people still have faith in the IAS as their last resort. The politicians are at a all time low level. The people never feel confident about the police force because of their high-handed practices and corruption. Of course, judiciary is one institution in which people are now reposing their confidence. However, judiciary doesn't cover the wide area of administration. Generally, poor people are out of reach of the judiciary. Therefore, IAS in spite of all their failings, still commands the faith and respect of the common people specially the poor ones.

However, the premier services themselves are reeling under the threat of their existence in view of globalization where the private actors, are calling the shots and they intend to control the governance on governments.

It is an accepted canon of psychology that the persons in group like bureaucrats will resist as a group when they fear change but they will also accept as a group if they are told about in advance, and can participate in setting up the new work routine and goals. Then they adopt new methods and achieve goals with surprising speed. Thus, growing in healthy psychology will help in preparing skilled bureaucrats.

Civil Servants in France

France lacks institutions and structure characteristics of parliamentarianism. Members of Parliament may put questions but this is a tame affair. In France there are no parliamentary committees of the type which exist in UK and in India. Civil Service has no interface with either chamber of the legislature. Therefore, when a politician of average ability ascend to the presidency, the civil servants also give output of average quality. The bureaucrats function generally invisibly and with utmost subtleness and silence. The civil servants are not restricted to administrative sector alone. They are sent on transfer to spend a term with private sector and even the political sector. The former Prime Minister of France, Jacques Chirac, was a civil servant on leave. They are sometimes called the Fifth Republic, a Republic of Civil Servants. Even then, the career in Civil Service is still one of the most sought after professional careers by young generation as it has variety, excitement and challenge.

Bureaucrats in Socialist Countries

After the radical changes in Central and Eastern Europe, in 1989, the Civil Service is being replaced with a permanent, professional and impartial Civil Service system, capable of serving a democratically-elected government in a liberal democracy. It is now non-committed to socialist ideology or to the communist party in power. The earlier was parallel party bureaucracy consisting of loyal party members, which developed policies, gave orders and controlled the State bureaucracy. It was politicization of the Civil Service. However, it was better than the bureaucracy in former authoritarian regimes in Spain and Portugal which used the military as their instrument of suppressions. However, lack of legal provisions protecting civil servants against political dismissal has undoubtedly created emotional imbalance among the civil servants who then naturally continued in the tradition of politicization after the change of regime in nine States i e the Russian Federation, Yugoslavia, Bulgaria, Hungary, Poland, the Slovak Republic, Estonia, Latvia and Lithuania.

In conclusion, the former politico-administrative systems left Central and East European countries with a legacy of politicization of recruitment and promotion systems, direct subordination to political parties, horizontal and vertical fragmentation and a tradition of extreme centralization of both policy-making and policy implementation. However efforts are on to make Civil Service impartial and permanent.

Marx believed in withering away the bureaucracy. He stated,

> "Certain mechanizing had developed within the State which were inseparable from it and which proved resistant to all rational argumentation, and that consequently, well meaning and indulgent criticism was quite senseless."[10]

According to him bureaucracy in itself becomes the final objective of the State i e the bureaucrats fends for themselves.

The Socialist China believes in cultural collectivism. The term collectivism refers to a constellation of psychological entities such as feelings, emotions, beliefs, ideology and actions. Thus, the Chinese system of bureaucracy is based on collective decision of party in power based on principles of enforcement of role behaviour, sharing of group responsibility and outcome, regulation of individual motivation and morality and conflict containment. However, Chinese individual is emerging as different Chinese societies have different faces.

Bureaucrats of Other Asian Countries

Asia has wide variety of psychology. There is a powerful intellectual movement of Islamizing knowledge including psychology. Japan shares to a large extent the perspective on management and organizational behaviour that have spread from China and India so also is the case of Thailand. The Filipinos give greater emphasis on the collective experiences of a people with a common bond of history, which is very specific to the Philippines. The Philippines had Spanish colonial bureaucracy which was based on patronage and retainership. They went for presidentialism in 1890s. So also South Korea chose the same presidentialism and patronage. Now it is moving towards an open presidentialist regime. There is heterogeneity with respect to demographic profiles, geographical and ecological features, ethnic and cultural backgrounds, and economic extremes and other diversities, yet the Asian perspective is distinct from the Western perspective with respect to the goals, content and methodology. The Asian psychology has greater concern for larger societal and personalities of life and existence. There is need for a blend of the two perspectives. It is time that the journey to the East begins.

> "In Pakistan, the civil bureaucracy has to some extent been checked by the military (another bureaucracy!) and martial law, but the situation there appears somewhat healthier from a democratic standpoint in the sense that judiciary is functioning to check the excesses of both the military and the civil bureaucracy."[11]

Bureaucrats in African and Latin American Countries

Psychology has to go native if it is to be creative and relevant to society, says BN Mukherjee.

The Latin American countries and African countries have nineteenth century presidentialist regimes which inherited their relatively weaker retainer bureaucracies from Spain and Portugal. Conscious of past abuses of executive power throughout Latin America, especially under authoritarian rules, strengthening the power of legislatures and imposing constraints on executive authority by making heads of government more accountable to national congresses, advocates through such controls as interpolation (in Peru) and impeachment (in Brazil and Venezuela). In Brazil and Chile, reconsideration of the parliamentary option is being worked out. Thus, semi-presidentialist solutions appear imminent. This is especially true in those cases where there were instances of human rights violations, a record of unrestrained police action, and previous experience with the lack of accountability of military and civilian bureaucrats for actions taken during authoritarian rule. The people were sceptical about the role of bureaucrats because they had alliances with military officials and perpetuated excesses. This caused fatigue in bureaucrats and they failed to take administrative measures for development and economic upliftment. One of the causes attributed is the weak national government in power. However, Brazil has moved from federal governments to the democracy in 1985 empowering its States and local governments. Sub-Saharan Africa is also moving from authoritarian bureaucracy to the responsible bureaucracy to respond to market reforms and democratization though the design of social and economic policies. In Africa, the bureaucrats are also trying to align with NGOs who are doing much of their jobs especially in countries with poor majorities. This is because of the established track record of many NGOs in effective service delivery in such areas as the distribution of food and medicines, care for abandoned children and creator of institutions better able to respond to the needs of the poorest of the poor. The international agencies under the auspices of the World Bank, ILO, UN Habitat and IMF are trying to reach services to the poor like updated land records through various multinational agencies engaged in this job to enlighten these countries of Africa to an appropriate administrative mechanism or technology as substitute to bureaucrats.

US Bureaucrats

The US Bureaucrats are more technical and experts than their counterparts in other countries. The American President has all powers to hire and fire them. The 'bashing of bureaucrats' has become a staple of contemporary politics. The Pendulum Act and the Civil Services Reforms Act (CSRA) of 1978 govern the bureaucrats in USA. But the 'spoilt system' is still prevalent in USA which can be defined as follows:

> Parties are necessary and organization is essential. It is the duty of the citizen ... to support the party that stands for right policies and to adhere closely to its official organization. Loyalty should be rewarded by appointment to positions within the gift of the party; and disloyalty should be looked upon as political treason. Positions constitute the cohesive force that holds the organization intact."[12]

After the Watergate scandal, the need was felt to make Civil Service more independent and impartial. The civil servants of USA are working in that direction who are now in between the committed bureaucrats of China and neutral and impartial bureaucrats of India. US has different type of bureaucratic set-up.

> "The Economic development of a society ... requires a breed of bureaucrats different (eg more free wheeling, less adhering to administrative forms, less attached to the importance of hierarchy and seniority) from the type of man who is useful when the primary concern of the bureaucracy is the maintenance of law and order (La Palombara)."[13]

The key to economic development lies in picking men with or in training them to have high achievement drives.

> "These men, in turn, will bring about the development.... The psychologist insists, as the businessman is apt to, that the most effective control on an economic development programme lies not in the excellence of the plan, as economists are apt to argue, but in the excellence of the men selected to carry it out. Some devices are needed both to select the best man to operate it and to eliminate or retain those who do not perform up to the standards."[14]

Thus, US prefers non-government, non-bureaucratic type of person to run US administration.

Controlled Bureaucrats in Scandinavian Countries

> "Five countries – Sweden, Denmark, Norway, Finland and New Zealand have established the office of Ombudsman. Germany has established a similar institution for military matters, and the British Parliament has been considering a parliamentary commission along similar lines. The office of Ombudsman, which appeared first in Sweden around 1809, constitutes a national civic watchdog, a complaint or grievance man, who provides protection to individuals against the government bureaucracy and its excesses."[15]

> "In New Zealand, out of 776 complaints filed, after investigations, 54 complaints were held to have been justified. About half of these were immediately rectified by the departments or agencies concerned."[16]

The power of the ombudsman rests with the public, which knows from day to day what he is doing. If he reprimands a policeman for being tough to a citizen, the newspapers publish the rebuke, and readers cheer. The ombudsman, the people feel, is their man.

Conclusion

An efficient bureaucrat means one who can administer known, established principles, rules and procedures. Small scale reforms and minor creativity will be exercised in a bureaucratic organization but these will relate to details or to the improvement of existing methods.

> "Because the work is repetitive and predictable, much can be done about simplifying, streamlining and mechanizing procedures.

> Nor will the trend stop with the assignment of the repetitive work to clerks and the development of forms and standard procedures and mechanized work passed from human hands to the claws of machinery or computer i e automated."[17]

In such an organization like bureaucracy, the innovators or creative type of person, faces following problems:

1. He will become bored and leave or he will divert his energies into hobbies or social services away from his job.
2. He will stifle creative urgings and lapse into apathy.
3. He will be forced by the *status quo* types who outnumber him and who knowingly or unknowingly combine against him.

In the fast growing world and in the age of liberalization and information technology, the *status quo* bureaucrats will also fail in a short time because they will not be able to keep pace with the changing scenario of the bureaucratic organization. Thus, bureaucrats always faces psychological strain and stress. In developing countries like India, they have three bosses i e political executive or minister, or elected representative like mayor or head of Panchayat, bureaucratic boss and the public. Some of the bureaucrats in the elected bodies like municipalities, Panchayats or local council or commune, have to work with the elected representatives who are not so predictable and permanent as their bureaucrat bosses. As a result, they change. If they can't change, they develop tension and imbalance in their personalities which is bad for a healthy organization. They have at times to compromise with their principles in life under pressure to continue in government jobs. The revolutionaries or the outspoken and straight-forward bureaucrats have to face wrath from their superior, obliqueness from the seers and disobedience or disrespect from the subordinates. Thus, bureaucrats have a difficult psychological challenge to maintain a proper balance in their personalities.

> "Synectics as theory holds that creative efficiencies (innovative skill) can be markedly increased if bureaucrats understand the psychological process by which they operate."[18]

The emotional component is sometimes more important than the rational. If one can appeal to the cultural, religious or charitable instinct of bureaucrats, the bureaucrats will be highly motivated and will later on prove successful. Thus, a leader among bureaucrats should understand the psychology of the groups well which may differ from society to society and from country to country. Therefore, study of psychology helps in proper understanding of bureaucrats as to how he will react to a given situation and secondly, how best he can be utilized for the good of the people and the country.

REFERENCES

1. Dyer Frederick C and Dyer, John M, *Bureaucracy Vs Creativity*, University of Miami Press, Cord Gables, Florida (USA), 1965, p 17.
2. Ibid, pp 21-22.
3. Ibid, p 33.
4. Ibid, p 21.
5. Agrawal, PK, *Motivation and Indian Bureaucracy*, MD Publications, New Delhi, 1995, p 65.
6. Ibid, p 67.

7. Parkinson, CN, "Excessive Controls and Bureaucracy" in *I am Sorry: Indian Bureaucracy at Crossroads*, Dr PK Agrawal and N Vittal (eds), Manas Publications, New Delhi, 2008, p 127.
8. Philip Davies, *Your Total Image: How to Communicate Success*, J Piathas Books, London, 1988.
9. Bagchi, Sanjay, *The Changing Face of Bureaucracy*, Rupa & Co, New Delhi, 2007, p 34.
10. Hegedus, Andras, *Socialism and Bureaucracy*, Allison & Bushy Ltd, London, 1976, p 12.
11. Ibid 1, p 133.
12 Thayer, Frederick C, "The US Civil Services: 1883-1993 (RIP)" in *Modern Systems of Government*, Ali Faraz Mand (ed), Sage Publications, California (USA), 1997, p 100.
13. Ibid 1, p 132.
14. Ibid, p 129.
15. Ibid, p 142.
16. Ibid, p 143.
17. Ibid, p 32.
18. Ibid, p 57.

2

Behaviour of Bureaucrats in India

Everybody interacts with bureaucrats either directly or indirectly. One has to know the psychology of the person with whom he is dealing with so that he can deal with him fruitfully. Psychology is a science which aims to give us better understanding and control of behaviour of bureaucrats. Let us analyse how the bureaucrats working in environment of different provinces in India behave differently based on their ethos, culture and background. Let us first take up how the bureaucrats in the Central Government think and behave.

Bureaucrats in the Central Government

India has a federal structure of polity like in USA. India is a vast country, geographically as well as administratively. The bureaucrats at the centre has to serve at present about 1,250 million citizens with varied castes, colour, creed and culture only next to China. The federal units are called States, unlike provinces elsewhere. There is a proper administrative division between the Centre and the States. Both of them are autonomous in their respective field. Their division of administrative work is earmarked through Union List (List I), State List (List II) and the Concurrent List (List III) as per Seventh Schedule of the Constitution of India.

As regards items under List III ie the Concurrent List, the Central Government has overriding power. All union territories are also administered by the Central Government. Thus, the Central bureaucracy derives overriding powers vis-a-vis State bureaucracy. Secondly, the States have been traditionally mismanaged in the past except one or two States, due to political interference and excessive corruption. As a result, their financial health is in disarray. Therefore, the States have to depend on the Central Government for their existence and running of administration. In view of multifarious functions covering UTs, States and even Panchayat bodies, the bureaucracy at the Centre is of a large size of about 4 million employees. Secondly, there are All India Services to unite the country due to past history of India. These services ie Indian Administrative Services, Indian Police Service and Indian Forest Service are also top ranking services in the States. Thus, seemingly, the bureaucracy at the Centre and the States are one and the same though working and serving for different bosses. They tend to look alike. The bureaucrats like other people in the society

(a) are product of the environment,

(b) want security,

(c) need bread and butter,

(d) are fundamentally lazy,

(e) are basically selfish,

(f) do what they have to do,
(g) are creatures of habits,
(h) are product of their heredity, and
(i) have to satisfy their needs.

Thus, like a case of any other person, the behaviour of a bureaucrat is inextricably intertwined with nature and nurture. As the Central Government is a large bureaucracy, it is very powerful and is indifferent, neutral and is inaccessible. It runs on the prescribed rules and regulations which are made for people as per citizen's perspective. The size of public bureaucracy is not increasing as per increase in the population.

> "About 86% of the Central staff in 2001 was concentrated in the Ministry of Railways, Defence, Posts and Home Affairs having central police organizations. Industrial workers constitute one fifty of the total strength and are covered by laws relating to industrial labour."[1]

A time will come when more amount will be spent on pensioners of bureaucracy than the active bureaucracy. The bureaucrats at the centre have lot of security emanating from Article 311 of the Indian Constitution and are covered by many statutes, regulations, rules and conduct rules made for them. IAS is called steel like service. This is too much secured. It is high time that this steel security has to be melted a little so that work output is more. It is well said that it is very difficult to take action against an official. Even an employee on contract service can challenge his removal in Court or Tribunal. In the process, the department or government body is more harassed than the employee concerned. Therefore, senior officers everywhere, avoid even initiating disciplinary proceedings, or departmental proceedings. The departmental heads are not so equipped with procedural requirements that they can punish a subordinate employee. As a result, the functioning in the Central Government depends on self-motivation of an employee. If he is himself motivated, he will perform his duties and even work for others, who are lazy and shirkers. In Central Government, one may not find his boss, peer or subordinates belonging to the same region, caste or community. Therefore, possibility of favouritism based on caste, region or community is remote though the employees complain that a South Indian favours the South Indian, a Bengali favours the Bengali and so on. Many a times, such allegations are baseless and are raised by the inefficient and corrupt officials to hide their misdeeds.

In the Central Government, the top bureaucrat ie Secretary is very powerful and it is very difficult to reverse his decision. His decision is based on many layers or hierarchies in bureaucracy and even having approval of minister before it is published. Therefore, there are many invisible decision-makers before his decision is made public. All those unite when his decision is challenged. It is the bureaucratic head who represents the government as far as rules of business is concerned and he is accountable to public as well as to Parliament. Therefore, he is supposed only to follow legitimate orders of the political executives. But sometimes, the bureaucrat conspires with the political executive or succumbs to the dictates of the political masters and from there the illegal chain of decisions starts. It is said that the financial stakes in the Central Government are quite high and therefore, the greedy politicians and bureaucrats hover around posts in the Central Government which are juicy or wet and ultimately are caught in the vigilance net or by the Central

Bureau of Investigation (CBI) for indulging in graft. Two such incidents have come in light recently known as 2G Scam or Coalgate Scam in which few lakh crore of rupees or millions of dollars were misappropriated by the nexus of the politicians/ ministers and senior bureaucrats. Even lower level officials were involved and their palms were duly greased. However, in these two scams, the bureaucrats for the first time in the history of India, were cautioned that they can be held up for their criminal acts of bribery and corrupt practices even after many years of their retirement ie they can be brought back from the graves. How can the bureaucrats take up this challenge at ease or lie low? The errors of investigations/ judgements made by the police officials in CBI gave fillip to fight back by the bureaucrats. Many innocent and known honest IAS officers were named in First Information Reports (FIRs) by the CBI. The public supported the bureaucrats vis-a-vis CBI because public has hardly any faith in police. Secondly, the CBI as a police organization is not concerned that the economy of the country has to be run smoothly with so many compromises. It is not a straight-forward regulatory function unlike in the past. Even the judges couldn't appreciate the predicaments of the bureaucrats to give room to the decisions by the bureaucrats to boost the sagging economy by involving the private sectors on their terms and conditions. As a result, the seniormost bureaucrats during UPA-II regime from year 2012 to early 2014 stopped taking decisions. This paralysis of decisions by bureaucrats cost UPA-II the defeat at hustings in 2014 and pro-bureaucrat Chief Minister of Gujarat Shri Narendra Modi was voted to power on his promise to regenerate or reassure the bureaucrats who can deliver results. Thus, bureaucrats function effectively and speedily when there is a clear mandate and the political master is prepared to own and in fact owns the responsibility of what he instructs them orally. Additionally, he should be able to protect them from vagaries of enquiries, media accusations or media trial and subsequent onslaught on their career even after retirement. These are many widely worded boundaries but a self-assured bureaucrat is the only surety to take prompt and fair decisions. Cautious or slow decision-making bureaucrats are out of pace and they will dig graves for themselves and for the system.

Thus, code of conduct are required to be rewritten for the bureaucrats in the light of fast moving age of information technology, globalization, economic and social developments. The old bureaucrats and the younger officers entering the government in recent years face moral dilemma in their working. The liberalized, global and competitive economy is bringing with it a bewildering array of unfamiliar problems, which have to be handled by a State with less sovereignty externally and less command authority internally. Thus, the bureaucracy which tried to enter into the kitchen of the citizen as a part of the welfare measure, is finding itself in dilemma, constraint or vicious circle due to crunch of funds because of increasing cost on its sustenance and price rise. The government is trying to pull out from the earlier welfare model, but it cannot do it due to possible political holocaust and public backlash on the streets and rural courtyard.

Secondly there is increasing commitment of the government towards rural poor and the urban poor to provide them at least 100 days employment in a year and a house for the homeless in urban areas apart from the food security to them. The bureaucrats are finding it difficult to generate funds for their political masters, due to sluggish economy all over the world except in China. In such adverse circumstances, it will be difficult to find bureaucrats to manage State affairs unless the political executives or politicians become rational and practical and do not indulge into creating rising expectations among public without backyard support from the revenue collection or economy. Thus, the bureaucrats function effectively in an environment in which the political executives are prepared to consider their advice and problems and are ready to be partners with the bureaucrats to implement their election promises in an objective fair and impartial manner. A tense bureaucrat is a problem for the system and also a burden to the society. Therefore, joint efforts are to be made to carry forward the mandate of the political party in power by the political executives and bureaucrats with rational and practical approach. Then only some good results can be delivered by the bureaucrats at the centre. The bureaucrats at the centre has day-to-day problems from the higher courts which deliver high sounding sermons in the form of orders or judgements in the country through Public Interest Litigations (PILs). This trend is catching up like infection up to District or Subordinate Courts. Few advocates disgruntled from the system come up to solve some long standing politico-social problem in their petitions by reading newspapers, media-news or social network sites or after study of problem or ailment in depth of the society. The courts hear them at the cost of normal list of cases and pass judgements in these matters bypassing long pending cases. The bureaucrats say that they do not have funds in the exchequer to honour all orders delivered in the PILs. The courts are not prepared to hear their constraints and feel that this is the normal way of bureaucrats saying 'no' to everything. As a result, the orders of courts and political executives remain unattended to because resources are not there to implement them. In such an awkward situation, one has to appreciate how the senior bureaucrats function in spite of threats from their political masters and masters in judiciary for contempt of court. The latter is a real threat and can mar his otherwise bright and smooth career and expectations in life for which he chose public service as a career even being the cream of the society during his student life.

The exercise of authority by the Central Government bureaucrats is subject to the scrutiny by Comptroller and Auditor General of India. The legislature is, of course, competent to debate any executive action and give directions through resolutions and committee reports.

In the broad backdrop of predicament of bureaucrats in the Central Government, let us survey how the bureaucrats function in various State Governments in India starting from Uttar Pradesh having about 180 million population.

Bureaucrats in Uttar Pradesh

State of Uttar Pradesh is bigger than most of the countries in the world both in respect of area and population. Therefore, bureaucracy of Uttar Pradesh is also of mega size and is very powerful one. The State had been dominating the Centre having the government of the same political party. Therefore, the bureaucrats from UP dominated the administration of the Central Government for many years. But for the last two decades, UP has been having government of the political party which was not at the Centre. Therefore, UP has lost its eminent position. The first two decades after Independence, UP saw fairly good governance with mature leaders like GB Pant, Sampurnanand and CB Gupta. Issues of democratic decentralization and reorientation of administration got raised, and the system was still coping. UP was, at the time, one of the few States in India which was devoid of violent issues.

> "It was however, in the watershed year, 1967, that the first serious salvo against the Congress was fired. A Sanyukta Vidhayak Dal (SVD) government was formed, and the period of political instability began in the State. Government came in and went out with increasing frequency. In a period of nine years (1967-76), UP had six Chief Ministers with four spells of President's rule. From 1977 onwards, following the lifting of the emergency, UP witnessed nearly 12 changes in government till 1997, with varying durations of the President's rule in between. Responding to the quick and unanticipated shifts in power structures, and the unfortunate deterioration in the political culture, cracks started appearing in the IAS collectively. Loyalties kept shifting and officers gradually began to be identified with different political parties, factions or individuals. For some cadre officers seeking the political umbrella became, at first, a convenient choice, and, for a smaller number, a necessity. In turn, the beneficiary hoped to succeed in enlisting powerful support. What was lost were the integrity, independence, objectivity, fairness and impartiality that constitute the essential strength of the Civil Service. At time, politicians and civil servants became ungrudging partners in manipulative, shady deals. In administration, one could observe the growing level of venality, self-interest, and self-aggrandisement (even to the extent of harming a service colleague) severe decline in professionalism, greater sycophancy, loss of neutrality and absence of transparency."[2]

Civil Service tenures have tended to become shorter and more uncertain, leading not only to lack of senses of involvement of the affected officers, but also to their sheer inability to acquire knowledge about a job, and to function effectively. Theoretically, transfer is not deemed as punishment. In actuality, an inconvenient transfer after a short duration posting can be highly traumatic. The family of the transferred officer suffers, children's education becomes a difficult problem, morale crumbles. How can the officer maintain his psychological balance and equilibrium? His behaviour becomes abnormal. He looks up at the headquarters at Lucknow rather than attending to local calls of his duty.

In this respect, the UP situation has developed into that of a chronic and acutely sick patient. Figures speak eloquently of the sorry pass to which things have come. It is estimated that during the last six years (1991-97) over three thousand IAS/IPS officers have been transferred. Table 2.1 summarizes the position.

The formal system of transfer is reported to be in shambles. Most of the proposals for transfers of IAS and other senior officers are said to emerge not from departments of the government charged with the function of preparing proposals (eg appointments, home etc) but from CM's office. If the press is to be believed, lists are handed down to the Secretaries concerned, and orders are issued on that basis. It is said that, in a large number of cases, the Chief Secretary is not even consulted. In as many as 37 districts, tenures have varied from 12 to 18 months, in 13 between 18-24 months, in 11 between 6-1 months, in 3 between 3-6 months, and in another 3 districts the period of postings have on an average been three months or less. These do not fully reflect the sharp deterioration of the more recent years. The 'transfer industry' is perhaps the only flourishing industry in the largest populated State of India

TABLE 2.1: Transfer of IAS/IPS Officers in UP from 1991-97

Period	Head of Government/ State	IAS officers transferred	IPS officers transferred
1. July 1991 to Dec 1992	Kalyan Singh (CM)	293	228
2. Dec 1992 to 2 June 1995	Mulayam Singh Yadav (CM)	321	493
3. June 3, 1995 to Oct 17, 1995	Mayawati (CM)	284	294
4. Oct 18, 1995 to Apr 3, 1996	Motilal Vora (Governor)	163	151
5. Apr 4, 1996 to Mar 20, 1997	Romesh Bhandari (Governor)	181	229
6. Mar 21, 1997 to Apr 20, 1997	Mayawati (CM)	207	151

Source: Indian Express, *Dainik Jagran*, Government announcements.

because officers are generally corrupt and make money on most of the posts. The politicians easily blackmail them and take the pie of their flesh.

The prevailing perception is that bureaucrats are used as pawns or tools by the party in power to settle scores with its rivals. Those considered to be loyal, pliable and convenient are utilized to focus resource uses on the programmes of the ruling party's preference in terms of the locations or predetermined sets of beneficiaries. Some say, senior officials are used even for raising party funds and 'plum' postings have to be paid for before being given. It is uncertain how a large State like UP will come out of its nightmare of political skulduggery, moral degradation and administrative corruption. Following the general trend in administration, the judiciary has also become corrupt and people in general talk of corruption even in social life and like to make fast buck by hook or by crook. The rampant corruption has weakened the spine of administration of the country.

Perceptions About IAS Officers (External, Internal)

The number of studies about IAS cadres in UP and other States is rather limited. CP Bhambri (1973), K Mathur (1973), E Eames and P Saran (1989), Prayag Mehta (1989), MA Mettalib (1992) and Bansal (1975) are some of the scholars who have carried out research relating to behavioural aspects of the Civil Services Personnel. These studies are limited in scope, and the sample sizes (where utilized in field research) are rather small. The general findings are that the Service is elitist in character, low in values of modernization, sticks to bureaucratic behavioural values of formal authority, is rule oriented, impersonal, and displays poor accessibility. It does not undertake risks, lacks initiative and is inadequate in responsiveness. Some, like Jain and Dwivedi (1990), have stated that "people evince an increasing concern and disappointment about the unhelpful attitude and lack of responsiveness from bureaucrats." The criticism is aimed at their 'self-perpetuating oligarchic actions'. In 1980, PS Appu, senior service officer himself, stated that the bureaucracy was demoralized and in a state of decay. Seshan used much harsher words denigrating civil servants for their lack of courage and tendencies of collusion and capitulation.

It has not become possible to lay hands on a survey based study about the IAS officers of the UP cadre. However, a detailed study on the basis of 289 responses from IAS officers and 528 from politicians, police officers, co-professionals, technocrats, academicians and other non-IAS categories has been carried out by P Singh and Asha Bhandarkar (1994), which throws light on the external and internal perceptions about IAS officers. The study used certain pre-determined and structured response-points regarding attitudes, behaviour and performance. Questionnaires numbering 40 were sent out to IAS officers of different deputation, 289 responded to the questionnaires who belonged to nearly ten State cadres, including 37 from UP.

Table 2.2 shows that for the response items (all have not been included here), in the eyes of co-professionals and non-

TABLE 2.2: External and Internal Perceptions about IAS

Response on items	Response from Non-IAS persons (N-528) (%)	Response from IAS officers (N-289) (%)
1. Projects self as an expert on most things	75	17.65
2. Concern focus on own career	68.94	21.54
3. Self Opinionated	66.29	8.65
4. Power Hungry	58.33	4.50
5. Shrewd and Manipulative	56.82	7.96
6. Procedure and rule focused	54.17	10.73
7. Arrogant	53.79	19.03
8. Inaccessible	48.11	22.49
9. Action and result focused	31.71	61.59
10. Intellectually high calibre	22.73	66.82
11. Trustworthy	15.53	48.44
12. Innovative/Creative	8.71	52.25
13. Visionary and Transformational	8.32	44.98

Source: IAS Profiles (P Singh and A Bhandarkar, 1994).

officials the image of the IAS is by and large negative, contrary to the self-perception of the officers. It is indeed surprising that nearly one-fifth of the IAS respondents concede that their focus of concern is on their own careers, that they are inaccessible and arrogant, and that they project themselves as experts in most things.

The study further reveals that Service Officers assign high value to improving their skills and capabilities, greater decentralization and delegation of authority, reduced political interference and clearly defined performance-reward linkages. On the other hand, they assign low value to risk taking and drastic changes in the system.

The IAS officers in UP believe in assiduity and prefer the doer style, but majority is reconciled to drifting with the current. As for difficulties experienced, the IAS officers, illustratively, articulate them as follows:

- Short tenures.
- Ad-hocism in policies.
- Irrational populism.
- Short life of governments and absence of continuity.
- Absence of support from superior officers.
- Too much of conformity.
- Insufficient power/authority.
- Heavy workloads.
- Political interference and pressures.
- Criminalization of politics.
- Corruption and nepotism.
- Political and social fragmentation.[3]

However, the IAS Officers Association in UP has rightly begun the purge. They have been, in their annual session voting most corrupt IAS officer in UP. Two such ex-Chief Secretaries ie AP Singh and Smt Neera Yadav who have been jailed, were listed as the most corrupt officers by the UP IAS Officers Association also.

The position of lower level bureaucracy is more degraded. Most of the State Civil Service officers are corrupt and the lower level clerks and inspectors etc are dipped in corruption up to the neck level. Even, most of judicial officers are corrupt directly or indirectly. When any officer is posted, the lower level bureaucracy shows a great amount of obedience and sincerity to him and in turn runs its usual corruption racket unabated.

The police in UP is thoroughly corrupt. Even recruitment in police is afflicted with corruption. The vigilance set up in UP is itself corrupt. The police personnel believe that they will obey the orders of the king whether these orders are right or wrong. For the district level police, the king is the head of party in power or nominee of the Chief Minister. Every official in UP thinks that his salary is his basic right. He has a right for money for whatever extra he does on duty. Now, the demand for bribery has gone so high that the other side of public is not able to oblige because quantum of bribe has to be always proportional to the advantage being given to the other side of the table. Earlier it used to be 5-10%. Now it extends up to 50-60% of the amount released from the government. In regulatory functions like police case and recruitment, there is no limit. Government jobs are only green pastures for corrupt officials instead of the places of performance of duties. As a result, the State has gone into decadence and is becoming one of the most backward State after Bihar whereas earlier it used to be among four major States in growth and per capita income. Industries have migrated or have been closed down. Only NOIDA and Ghaziabad are flourishing being near to Delhi in NCR region. The State is crumbling under backlashes of castes, creeds or religion. It is hoped that people will give a heavy and final blow to the politics of caste or community and corrupt politicians of past and present including their crony bureaucrats will be behind bars in times to come. Then only, the behaviour of the bureaucrats will be commensurate with the professional requirement as per standards of services laid down.

Bureaucracy in Bihar

Like UP, the bureaucrats in Bihar are also corrupt and caste-ridden. They are lazy, egoistic and are not forward-looking. UP bureaucracy is at least not so lazy. The bureaucrats in Bihar have surrendered to the politicians in spite of latest Nitish Kumar regime to regenerate it. They don't allow grassroot bodies like Panchayats to function in collusion with the Ministers who don't want to share their power and authority whatsoever small is left with them, with the Panchayati Raj Institutions. Therefore, the Supreme Court had to hold in one of the cases before it that even the President Rule can be imposed in the State for non-election of PRIs in the State of Bihar. Once the powerful Chief Minister Lalu Prasad Yadav had given the message to the country that the politics is a game of mockery of showing false dreams by appealing to the ego of people. There is no need of solid development work or transparent regulatory functions. Arrest of Lalu Prasad in the

Fodder Scam along with some bureaucrats from all levels has given a salutary message that corruption will be exposed one day or the other. Bureaucrats have started looking backward after this episode. Many ill-gotten properties belonging to bureaucrats have been auctioned and schools have been opened in those buildings. The bureaucrats at all levels in Bihar are now slowly realizing that corruption is not always a good bargain. But it is too late now. The social fibre of the society is broken. The caste divide is final. It is very difficult to retrace back. But with the change of wind at the Centre, people of Bihar want to experience the development wind and will not be carried away by cheap slogans of caste or religion. Appeal to religious sentiments has not made available two meals a day to the poor Muslims. The bureaucrats are now having more free hand. Mafia has been controlled. Incidents like murder of a Collector will not be there because those accused have been duly punished nor the Superintendent of Police will be killed again because the illegal coal mining had got jolt afterwards. The wife of bureaucrat not longer will be raped because the politician's son has since been jailed and the political future of her mother had eclipsed since then. Thus, the bureaucrats in Bihar have a mixed experience of working. Now a bureaucrat will not have to vacate his berth in Railway Coach in Bihar territory because the concerned MP is still facing the judicial trial for the same offence outside Bihar ie in West Bengal. Honest, straightforward and people-oriented bureaucrats had never had any problem in working in Bihar like any other places. They are respected, supported and remembered by people after their transfers including majority of politicians except few crooks who are in each class of people. However, it is a great challenge before the bureaucracy in Bihar to take Bihar at par with other States in India in the 21st century in spite of caste-ridden, corruption-loving and lazy society of Bihar. As all great reformers came from Bihar, all is not lost. The sun always rises from the east and Bihar is in the east of India.

Bureaucrats in Jharkhand

Jharkhand has been carved out of the erstwhile State of Bihar. It has poor legacy of Bihar. Over and above, due to local sentiments, the tribal Chief Minister is a preference in Bihar. But successive tribal Chief Ministers in Jharkhand from various political parties have done no good to the new State. Corruption is thriving in Jharkhand. There is hardly any accountability of the bureaucracy. There is no statesman among new leaders. There is no will to solve Naxalite problem. Even land reform measures for tribals have not been initiated. Hopefully, in such a vacuum of political leadership, conscious bureaucrats will come up and will win the hearts of simple people of Jharkhand including politicians and put the new State on the track of development which is very rich in the mineral resources. And therefore, industrialists are flocking to Jharkhand to set up industrial units in Jharkhand provided a stable and fair bureaucratic structure can be in place which is the responsibility of bureaucrats. The senior bureaucrats from the IAS are well-trained and are skilled in the art of development provided there is least unnecessary interference in performance of their duties.

There were many scandals of corruption involving Chief Ministers and down the line in the newly created State of Jharkhand. It has a poor legacy but it had lot of time to come out of the bad legacy of Bihar. It is not understood why so many tribal Chief Ministers who advocated for separate State on the plank of welfare of tribals, are not involving themselves in concrete works for the welfare of the tribals. The bureaucracy got demoralized. It is hoped that action in many corruption cases against high-ups will bring motivation among lower rank bureaucrats for sincere, honest and hard work.

Bureaucrats of West Bengal

The West Bengal bureaucrats recollect golden experience with the first Chief Minister Dr Bidhan Chandra Roy who laid the foundation of industrial development of West Bengal. Then, Siddhartha Shankar Roy was a tall figure who tackled Naxalism in the State in late nineteen sixties and early seventies by his militant leadership. He was very intelligent, quick decision-maker and believed in results but his drawback was that he believed in a committed bureaucracy which led to his downfall. Then, the Left Front Government came in power in 1977 and continued in power up to 2011. The bureaucrats were very happy and psychologically very stable because Jyoti Basu, the Communist Mughal, was very considerate and an experienced freedom fighter. He entrusted the control of bureaucracy to his senior colleague in party late Shri Binay Krishna Chaudhary, the Land and Land Reforms Minister who was lodged in jail for fourteen years during freedom struggle and was a saint of land reforms. The message was very clear to the bureaucrats that they.shouldn't fiddle with the interests of the pattadars and bargadars (sharecroppers) and should assist the government in implementation of land reforms, as key mandate of the Left Front Government. The bureaucrats under D Bandyopadhyay,

IAS, rose up to the expectations. The Panchayats were also formed at three levels and were entrusted with most of the powers of the governance. Initially, the bureaucrats and MLAs resisted as they were becoming powerless. But seeing no other alternative, bureaucrats compromised and transferred their power in various fields including land reforms, education, food supplies, employment generating schemes, housing schemes etc to Panchayati Raj Institutions or bodies including fund. The Chief Minister Jyoti Basu never criticised the bureaucrats and publicly declared that bureaucracy is like the water which changes shape according to the glass. On the other hand, he always asked his party cadres not to forgo their struggle culture and they should get their demands met from bureaucracy after agitation and movements. Things easily got, are easily lost. Thus, he never allowed his partymen to be rulers and always rebuked them whenever there was some problem or infraction in administration as he had devolved all powers to them through Panchayats and elected municipalities. He never bothered about the personal life of bureaucrats. Even he overlooked many sex-scandals by the bureaucrats. While the IAS Association of West Bengal met him with some demands, he said. "You have to yourself concede to the demands. I have no objection. Settle among yourselves." He knew well that due to departmental differences, the IAS officers themselves will oppose many of their demands when they sit as Secretaries of their respective departments. He always said, "As Chief Minister, I don't have power even to appoint a peon." Such was his probity and respect to the system. Though some people blamed him to favour his son, but he never explicitly asked for any favour to him. During the last days of his life, he made only one request to the State bureaucrats to regularise his cook which they happily did. He died without leaving any wealth behind him. His party CPI(M) had its association/union in the bureaucracy which was so powerful that most of their demands got fulfilled through the members of the Association. The senior bureaucrats were placed with only legitimate proposals which they found easy to approve. In this environment, the bureaucrats had nice time with their families. They were not disturbed at odd hours. At every level including police, there was a party nominee who would interact with the officer or office or police station. However, his allies in Forward Bloc and to some extent RSP continued to behave in usual manner as elsewhere in the country but their ministers were only two or three which the honest bureaucrats were asked to tackle. His successor Chief Minister, was trained by Shri Jyoti Basu for a long time as his Home Minister. After he assumed office, he followed the same line and behaved nicely with bureaucrats but later on he grew in ego and couldn't control the party cadres who became corrupt. Thus, Left Front Government was overthrown by the fiery Chief Minister Ms Mamta Banerjee who initially wanted to take revenge but didn't find much substances against any of the minister or bureaucrat. Now, in the regime of uncertainty, the bureaucrats are very perplexed and have become indifferent. The time will only tell how Ms Mamta Banerjee will take the bureaucracy along to make a better West Bengal.

Odisha Situation

The bureaucrats in Odisha are as easy going as the State is. The bureaucrats don't have mantle to change the working environment of the State. They can only contribute some positive results with their personal efforts and can introduce some reforms. The tribal populated State (22.5%) is basically devotee of Lord Jagannath and poverty prevails in far off areas of forests where tribals live. Their Panchayat representatives are also not so active. As a result, mining and forest mafia exploit the tribals. Few bureaucrats had resisted. One of them had to commit suicide under pressure from the mining mafia. Many of the bureaucrats were punished by arbitrary transfers. Some of them have acquiesced in the unholy nexus of politician and mining mafia and joined them in looting the State. There is not much motivation among the bureaucrats to work for the landless and sharecroppers in rural Odisha. They only want to serve either at Bhubaneswar or at New Delhi. The bureaucrats are elite in Oriya society and are highly respected. But time is not far off when their inaction and lack of devotion to their duties will be exposed before the public. After the kidnapping of Malkangiri Collector by the Naxalite in February 2011, there is a general panic among bureaucrats to be posted and transferred to Naxal affected districts though Chief Minister conceded most of the demands of Naxalites to secure release of the Collector, a devoted IAS officer from the South India. Some NGOs have joined in the so-called public issues. But only half of it is true. Many of them take money from the industrialists or mining operators and go into oblivion. Therefore, job of bureaucrat is very difficult. He doesn't have support from the subordinate staff or officers because of lack of knowledge and initiative on their part. Bureaucrats in Odisha have to work at all levels. After the gherao and manhandling of the most popular Chief Minister late Shri Biju Patnaik by Secretarial Union and Staff, none dares to take up a direct show down with the government staff.

Thus, there is lot of need for improvement in thinking and behaviour of bureaucracy in Odisha.

Forward-Looking Bureaucrats of Andhra Pradesh and Telangana

As one of the south Indian States, officials of Andhra Pradesh continue to be hard-working, obedient, forward-looking and devoted to their duties. Things have not changed after the division of the Andhra Pradesh into AP and Telangana on 2nd June 2014. Political division cannot effect cultural division. Culture is of permanent nature and has been matured after flow of incidents for centuries.

The law-abiding people and hard-working farmers have brought unpredictable prosperity to Andhra Pradesh. As a result, Andhra Pradesh has become surplus State in rice, chilli, tamarind, grapes, eggs, fish, etc from being a chronically deficit State. Its NRIs have, on the other hand, flooded the State with their bulk of remittances in dollars specially from the software sector of USA. As per the estimate, Andhra Pradesh alone had the State domestic product at US $37 billion in 2012-13.

The bureaucrats are not left behind. They have stood shoulder to shoulder with the local populace and have co-operated with leaders having mass base irrespective of the political party in power. The bureaucracy worked under various Congress governments. They also worked under the film idol late NT Rama Rao as the chief minister who used to call the bureaucrats for meetings at his residence office at 3 AM in the morning and often misbehaved with senior bureaucrats. But the bureaucrats did not notice discrimination or misbehaviour at the ground level or even at their work-place. Even some non-AP bureaucrats have emerged as leaders in the field of land records and survey. So they tolerated the misbehaviour because NT Rama Rao was virtually adored by the masses in the erstwhile united Andhra Pradesh. His representative Shri Chandra Babu Naidu also believed in good governance and introduced many innovations in Andhra Pradesh like e-governance.

After NT Rama Rao, politician administrator Shri YSR Reddy became a very popular Chief Minister due to his grassroots level jobs like construction of irrigation dams, distribution of lands among the tribals and the poor, etc. He specially got distributed lands to the tribals in those areas where the Naxalites had raised demands. He believed in meeting all demands of the people whereas the bureaucrats tend to question the demand on some pretext or the other. He used to visit districts personally and ensured proper implementation of developmental schemes. But his death while visiting one of the districts, in a plane crash put a stop on deep administrative reforms. However, his keen understanding and prompt handling of demands of Naxalites brought the Naxal movement in Andhra Pradesh to a halt which had seen the most fierce encounters as compared to other Naxal-affected States in India. Telangana has inherited some of the Naxalite-affected districts. The new government in Telangana has this great test in hand which if not handled properly, may derail their development initiatives.

There is a revolutionary change through AP Land Licensed Cultivators Act, 2011 which allows all the tenants who are not registered to take advantage of crop loan. A special machinery has been created to implement evictions of the non-tribals in illegal occupation of tribal lands and also to restore such lands to tribals. This will help to contain Naxalism in both States.

After the division, the separatist leader and the present Chief Minister of Telangana Shri K Chandrashekar Rao is expected to follow in footsteps of his worthy predecessors. As such, no separatist leader barring few exceptions had been successful administrators. They tend to become quite dictatorial and self-centred because of their long struggle. However, they should shed off their agitational tag and should be democratic in approach. Shri KC Rao has a good administration and permanent Civil Service at his disposal which can guide him while toeing his line and prove the thesis wrong.

It is hoped that both the States will prosper side by side. Shri Chandra Babu Naidu will use his earlier mantle of being a good administrator and will establish the new State of Andhra Pradesh to its old glory. In Andhra Pradesh, the bureaucracy is led more by the political elite than the administrative executives in implementation of development schemes specially with the help and co-operation of strong and active Panchayati Raj Institutions in place.

Work Culture-Oriented Bureaucrats of Tamil Nadu

Though the bureaucracy on the face seems to be divided between DMK and ADMK who take the reins of the State turn by turn invariably. Yet the administrative machinery is kept intact with sincerity and honesty. Though corruption is fast creeping into the vitals of the lower level officials partially because of bad example of Chief Ministers, yet they come on duty in time, make long and correct notes and do not bunk the office hours. They are not only obedient and sincere to their superior officers but are also equally helpful to the public or customers. It is due to this inherent strength of the State bureaucracy that industrialist, MNCs and IT companies are flocking to Tamil Nadu in spite of extra expenditure to be incurred by these companies on keeping the air-conditioning in work-place in order. The Tamil Nadu Police is also known for its discipline in other parts of the country. Similarly, the clerks in Tamil Nadu are considered most efficient and are preferred throughout the country. If corruption at the top can lessen, the bureaucracy will brighten at the lower level proportionately.

Rule-Bound Bureaucrats of Kerala

The State has achieved 95% literacy. The State is quite advanced in availability of health and education facilities. The lower level bureaucrats are proud of their work and do not pay any extra respect to their superior or bosses. The feudal bureaucrats have problem in Kerala as government facilities or perquisites are not available to them except salary and allowances. But there is work-culture from 10 AM to 5 PM. The bureaucracy is an enlightened one and will not tolerate underhand dealings by the senior officers. Their work-culture is more reflected when they host the tourists in Kerala. The police and lower level inspectors and clerks are also more or less corruption free. But the bureaucrats feel demeaning as compared to the haves of dollars from the gulf countries. Time is not far when this effect may catch up with lower level bureaucracy and they may gradually indulge into corruption. There is partnership leadership by the political executives especially during Congress regimes. It is now on the bureaucrats how they can continue up to the expectation of public for the good of all.

Pro-Reform Bureaucrats of Karnataka

The bureaucracy of the State has shown due openness and has converted Bangalore City as the Indian Seatle of USA. Revolution of IT sector has informed all sections of the society. As a result, making of software is a cottage industry. Basically, people and bureaucrats are open and helpful. IT majors like Infosys and WIPRO have reached a definite message to the State bureaucracy that either they change or perish. Naturally, they are following management principles which are being followed by the India's major IT companies.

(i) Be fast or leave the job.

(ii) Follow international trends and appropriate technology.

Thus Karnataka, though of late afflicted with corruption in mining of iron ore, the State maintains its work output and people-oriented bureaucracy.

It is hoped that despite failure to mobilise more people in spreading the message of integrity and efficiency, the bureaucrats of Karnataka continue to be efficient and expeditious decision-makers.

Small Size Bureaucracy of Goa

Goa is the smallest but the richest State in India. It has the highest per capita income due to foreign tourists. Even Chief Minister himself behaves like a bureaucrat. There are not many effective decentralized bodies of local administration. Therefore, delivery of services to the public depends as to how efficient, effective and honest Chief Minister is. In India, the cycle is there from dishonest to honest rule and vice-versa. Thus, at least India doesn't slip down to the hell. It continues, where it is though as per advances elsewhere, it should make its place in the country of advanced nations. The people are law-abiding. The foreign tourists couldn't spoil its social fabric. Goa maintains its social and cultural identity. Though most of the Goanese are Christian, they look alike with other Indian Hindus and Muslims. After the lifting of embargo on iron mining, by the Supreme Court, Goa is likely to enter into the new phase of development and prosperity. But challenge remains how Goa can protect its sea beaches and its fragile ecology from the onslaught of huge influx of tourists specially the foreigners and the Indians who find it a safe tourist destination specially in winter season. The bureaucrats will have these challenges before them in future. Goa is forerunner in the field of health facilities and peaceful law and order situation. Even the powerful journalist of all India stature couldn't be spared for his trivial offence of molestation by its law-abiding police and courts.

Development-Oriented Bureaucrats of Maharashtra

The public bureaucracy was helpful in the development of co-operative societies in the field of sugarcane. However, it failed to solve the problems of cotton growers and high rates of suicides by farmers in the Vidarbha region of Maharashtra. The bureaucrats in general have led the State on the path of modern advances in the fields of industries, service sector etc.

As a result, Mumbai, its capital, has developed as financial capital of India. One can observe its distinct work-culture where one visits or interacts with any office in Maharashtra including Municipal Corporation, Municipality or Panchayat offices. The outsider bureaucrats have contributed in the growth of Mumbai and Maharashtra which is recognized by all and sundry except by the few separatist and regional parties who want to exploit fragile sentiments of the Marathis by taking up these non-issues as major issues. People are hard-working and well-informed. A clerk will render help to the public man which will be done by an officer in other States.

However, English still rules in the official communications. It is likely that Hindi will replace English along with Marathi in near future. Maharashtra is going to lead India in the areas of media, advertisements, movies, industries and financial transactions from Mumbai. Hopefully, prosperity of Mumbai will trickle down to the districts and rural areas by the well concerted efforts of the Maharashtra bureaucracy.

Ideal Bureaucrats of Gujarat

After independence, statutes were enacted to implement Panchayat system of decentralized administration in many States of India. The bureaucracy of many States did not cooperate in connivance with the political executives to wield unhindered power by them. But the bureaucracy of Gujarat helped to grow up co-operative societies like milk cooperatives such as Amul and the Panchayati Raj Institutions in letter and spirit since the beginning which was done by West Bengal and Kerala in the year 1978 after Left Front Governments came into power with thumping majority there.

However, Maharashtra is a neighbouring State which has closely followed in the footsteps up Gujarat. As a result, Gujarat has always been a well-administered State and has been the first choice of new entrants to IAS who believe in good governance. There was hardly any intake in IAS and other All India Services from Gujarat as the Gujaratis are more inclined towards business and overseas ventures. However, the outsider bureaucrats who have made Gujarat their homes, worked devotedly and ensured that Gujarat progresses by leaps and bounds with their innovations and freedom of work. Following, general psyche of people, the administrators in Gujarat also became output-oriented which is a lesson to be learned by rule and procedure bound bureaucracy in other States. The people also duly respected bureaucrats.

It is a pleasure to interact with a general public servant in Gujarat who is very responsive and helpful unlike public servants elsewhere in the country. This is one of the reasons why Gujarat has made unprecedented progress in India and people from all States are flocking to Gujarat for jobs. Gujarat has attracted maximum Foreign Direct Investment (FDI). The country is now watching whether the present Prime Minister Shri Narendra Modi can implement Gujarat Model of progress in other parts of India which are plagued with lack of motivation, excessive dependence on Government grants and lack of work-culture. Gujarat's three term Chief Minister Shri Narendra Modi is also trying to infuse work-culture in bureaucracy of India. The bureaucrats always loved the systematic working of decentralized administration in Gujarat at all levels of Panchayat bodies, municipal bodies, micro-finance co-operatives and milk co-operatives. The system is so well-stabilized and defined that everyone works within its jurisdiction and there is mutual control.

In offices, the clerks do not go to get the files approved by officers which should be normally done by them. Everybody takes proper and quick decision at his level or pushes file upward. There are not many complaints by bureaucrats of political interference or undue pressure. As a result, there has been tremendous outstanding achievements by individual bureaucrats in their respective fields and the State in general. The political executives have traditionally provided freedom to bureaucrats to function and to experiments and they have maintained their faith. The level of integrity among bureaucrats of Gujarat is one of the highest in India. The bureaucrats made the dirtiest cities like Surat and other cities as the cleanest cities and the dirtiest river like Sabarmati as the cleanest river in the country apart from increasing the business manifold and per capita income as one of the highest in the country, reaching electricity, water supply, education and health facilities to every village and industries are scattered all over the State without any exception. It has been and is now as the most peaceful State after Godhra killing and subsequent communal riots in February-March 2002. One can find many Muslim constables in Gujarat police whereas in other States, Muslims get only catchy slogans to capture votes but the politicians forget their promises after winning the elections. Similarly, the tribal villages in Gujarat now have 24 hour electricity and safe drinking water. Irrigation water from Sardar Sarovar Dam has reached all nooks and corners of Gujarat. Even, the areas of Rann of Kutch and district of Bhuj which were chronically known for shortage of water, have now plenty of drinking water. Of course the story of Gujarat is bright because the bureaucrats and local population work hand-in-hand. The local population have the culture to be self-dependent. The NGOs and local charitable organizations are so well spread, equipped and resourceful that the government agencies have only to play a secondary role in normal times as well as during emergency situations. For this, Gujaratis settled abroad are to be thanked because they send lot of remittances of their hard-earned dollars.

I am sure that Gujarat is providing us some thoughts to ponder over.

Feudal Bureaucrats of Rajasthan

The public bureaucracy has inherited the feudal legacy of erstwhile Kings and Maharajas of Rajasthan. They have self-aggrandisement for no reason. They should have introspection rather than show of aristocracy and superiority. The public is loyal and obedient to its present Rajas or Maharajas as *Maibaps* (mother-father). This wrong syndrome has spoiled the psychology of bureaucrats and is responsible for their downfall as well as lack of improvements in administration. This is the reason why death figures of senior bureaucrats after the age of retirement at 60 years is the highest in Rajasthan. The bureaucrats feel frustrated and dejected because none attends their 'durbar' or them after retirement. The administration has not exploited the tourism potential of Rajasthan fully like small States of Kerala and Goa though it has the highest potential of promotion of tourism. There is some achievement of literacy among masses but lot is still required to be done on health and education fronts. The State had lot many scandals whereas the Ministers had exploited female staff or nurse in the State. However, due to plantation and check dam schemes State is getting normal rains and may wash out its misnomer as rainless State.

Aristocrat Bureaucrats of Punjab

The State is very rich and is foodgrains bowl of India along with neighbouring State of Haryana. If Punjab and Haryana will not produce, many Indians will die of hunger. This is due to hard-working people of Punjab who have left their mark all over the world. However, the bureaucracy in Punjab is reverse of the people. Though they had controlled militancy in nineteen eighties in Punjab but that leadership didn't continue for long in all fields. This shows that the State bureaucracy has unlimited potential but this is to be properly guided and harnessed. The bureaucracy has to control corruption within it which is now eating into its vitals. If there is good administration, religious fanaticism will disappear. Similarly, implementation of land reforms in this feudal State can bring in equity and higher production in agriculture field. For that, the senior bureaucrats have to take lead by their example.

Output-Oriented Bureaucracy of Haryana

It is surprising that in the same Secretariat of Punjab and Haryana, the rooms of Haryana bureaucracy thrive with expeditious disposal of works. If one rings to any official in Haryana, there will be a prompt and positive reply. Everybody will try his best to help though some corruption will be involved in the process. In this way, Haryana has gone long way to develop its fringe areas of Delhi like Gurgaon and Faridabad. After the imprisonment of Chautalas, one time most nefarious and powerful politician and Chief Minister, in the case of recruitment of school teachers, a better sense of respect to rules and fair deal is infused among incoming political executives of Haryana. As a result, State bureaucracy will take the State to higher level of progress and prosperity.

Indifferent Bureaucracy of Jammu and Kashmir

The State of Jammu and Kashmir has been suffering from Pakistan-sponsored terrorism for last three decades. However, the bureaucracy has properly demonstrated its mettle and strength to bear the brunt of it and fight against the armed militancy in Jammu and Kashmir. Many members of field level bureaucracy including police constables and officers have been killed. Even then, they are fighting all out war with sincerity and patriotism. But the State bureaucracy in the process becomes quite linked with army which is generally in martial law administration. Whenever there had been good administration like during the period of Ghulam Nabi Azad as Chief Minister, the militancy was at its lowest ebb as local support to the militants had in the process dried up. Thus good administration is the panacea of all ills in the country which is in the hands of public officialdom. There had been lot of inflow of the central aid to the State. If all the Central grants and aid can be fully and properly utilized in J&K, the State will enter into new era of peace and progress. For that, the bureaucracy has to wake up from its slumber and lead from the front in spite of loss of life for development.

Status of Bureaucrats in Madhya Pradesh

Initially, Madhya Pradesh was a backward State. The people are docile, good and amenable to the dictates of administration. The bureaucrats were given lot of free hand in the State. But the lower level bureaucracy from clerks to the inspectors has exploited the people like anything. Their misdeeds are coming into light now and then when the Lokayukta of Madhya Pradesh conducts raids and recovers lot of immovable and movable properties of the inspector level officials. It becomes an eye opener to the country how blatantly the lower level bureaucrats have exploited the people whom they were supposed to serve free of cost. In these raids, their properties are seized until accounted for and they are arrested. Though in few cases, there may be high-handedness of the State but it is the befitting reply to the high-handedness by the officials. The bureaucrats are taking undue advantage of less educated and simple public of the State. However, the State has become now one of the front row progressive States in the country. It is expected that bureaucrats will realize adverse consequences of corruption including their persecution, mental harassment and seizure of their properties and will contribute in the progress of the erstwhile backward State of Madhya Pradesh.

Inefficient Bureaucracy of Chhattisgarh

The State is surplus in power, revenue and mineral resources. In the new State, the bureaucrats have still to learn how to transact government files properly. Since inception, there is lot of improvement yet lot of additional training is required at lower tiers of the bureaucrats.

Secondly, it is high time that their proneness towards bribery is stopped in bud. In spite of an honest Chief Minister for last ten years, his Ministers continue in the same way as earlier Ministers in the Congress regime. The bureaucracy also doesn't facilitate new developments but acts as regulatory administration. They have to be proactive to progress and development of the State which has requisite potential to develop.

Sleepy Bureaucrats of Uttarakhand

The State is trying to come out of her bad legacy of corruption, nepotism and red-tapism of UP. During the 2013 flood havoc on hills at Kedarnath and nearby areas, it was evident that its separation has not yielded results. In such emergency situation, to be part of a larger State is a better option. Secondly, services have not reached the doorsteps of the common man nor the official red-tapism has reduced. The Chief Secretary or the Principal Secretary is as inaccessible as he was in UP. It is hoped that Panchayats in remote hill terrain, will take the rein, in their hands and take the State ahead.

Delhi and Other UTs

Administration of UTs have been always good as it has less political interference. The UTs have surplus central grants and have locational advantages for industrial development. But the bureaucratic delays and long procedures mar the advantage gained. There is hardly redressal of public grievances. The senior bureaucrats are either very scared to take action against their subordinates or are in league with them. The Ministry of

Home, Government of India, which is the nodal ministry for the UTs, has failed to streamline their working. Thus, public fail to believe that bureaucracy without political bosses is a better option in India.

Unstable Bureaucrats of North-Eastern States

Two States suffer from militant organization demanding separation from India ie Manipur and Nagaland. There is problem of local versus outsiders. The bureaucracy has yet to win the hearts of people. They are unable to utilize central grants fully and properly. As a result, the people are dissatisfied as their needs are not properly addressed. Corruption has increased and militancy has flourished on the basis of corrupt money. The militants also extort money from bureaucrats gained by them as corruption. However, bureaucracy has been fighting militancy with utmost neutrality, bravery and sincerity with the help of armed forces and has developed requisite infrastructure. It seems that the new era of peace and prosperity will be on the anvil in these seven sisters within next five years. Out of these, Sikkim and Tripura are already peaceful.

Traditional Bureaucracy of Assam

Like North-Eastern States, Assam is also afflicted with militancy and corruption. However, Assam's bureaucracy has shown pragmatism by development of industries in the State and updating its revenue records. Lot of infrastructure has also been developed and the State has its own resources to fight militancy. However, resilience of the State's bureaucracy has setbacks now and then when a serious incident of violence occurs involving either the locals and Bangladeshi Muslims or the tribals claiming for separate Bodoland. However, constant development initiatives by the bureaucracy can get over the separatist, communal and militant elements. It is the dissatisfaction of the local people which fuels these flare ups. Satisfied public is the greatest asset to the administration. It is hoped that better administrative measures will be taken at all levels of bureaucracy.

Concluding Remarks

We thus find on survey of all Indian States and the functioning of the Central Government that motivation is lacking writ large in government organizations. Motivation is mainly psychological. It refers to those forces operating within an individual or bureaucrat which impel him to act or not to act in a certain way. Behaviour is thus outward manifestation of motivation. Carrot and stick approach is no longer an accepted ideological framework. Money matters a lot. There is requirement of proper macro environment for work. If one finds himself midst law and order problem and traffic jams, he cannot give optimum output at his work place. Similarly, lack of objective personnel policy, frequent transfers or promotions based on favouritism will de-motivate government employees. There should be proper working environment at the work-place. The government offices now suffer from proper upkeep. Even in police station, stationery is not available to record complaints or FIRs. There is a need for good leadership. In India self-example motivates a lot.

Therefore, superior officers or political executives, ministers, Panchayat heads or Chairman of municipal bodies, have to conform their own conduct beyond any doubt in a free, fair and transparent manner. There are other factors like families, reference groups, formal or informal groups or social class which form one's personality. These psychological factors of bureaucrats are not being reconciled or integrated with the goals, objectives and processes of the government organization. Wherever, it has been achieved, the success rate is very high.

If we want responsive bureaucracy in India, the new work-culture should be fostered which should spring from the Indian psyche and not to be borrowed from outside. It is unfortunate that the Indian bureaucracy is falling into the trap of an independent or isolated organization unconcerned with people's needs and aspirations to whom they are to serve. They want to serve themselves which is uncalled for. Pandit Jawaharlal Nehru, the beloved Prime Minister of India criticized the ICS, the predecessor service of IAS as follows:

> "The good of India meant to them primarily the good of their own service. They formed a kind of mutual admiration society and were continually praising each other."[4]

It was Indira Gandhi who gave call for a 'committed bureaucracy' and during the internal emergency (1975-77), the politicization of the bureaucracy became even more intense:

> "By the end of the 60s, late Prime Minister Mrs Indira Gandhi destroyed the concept of an independent and a political Civil Services – career advancements were made in favour of civil servants committed to the authoritarian rule of the leader. Those who asserted their independence or remained apolitical were quietly sidelined and the opportunities in the Civil Services started making tacit alliances with politician."[5]

The same trend is visible at least in Uttar Pradesh and Tamil Nadu at present. The Shah Commission which was constituted to examine the Emergency excesses, came to the sad conclusion that some members of the service who were asked to bend, actually crawled.

Atal Bihari Vajpayee, an ex-Prime Minister observed in 1996 –

> "India rightly boasted of having a great asset in its permanent but non-political and impartial Civil Service. Sadly, the rot has set in here too. Casteism, Corruption and politicization have sapped the integrity and efficiency of our system of Civil Service."[6]

Shri NC Saksena, the ex-Director, Lal Bahadur Shastri National Academy of Administration observed:

> "The IAS has generally been indifferent to the resources that sustain the livelihood needs of poor. This is reflected in the way IAS officers grade their jobs. Industrial and commercial departments and corporation posts are highly sought after. The lowest ranked jobs are tribal and social welfare, revenue administration, land reforms, urban slums and rural development."[7]

Thus the fall in behaviour of the senior bureaucrats is very steep. It is high time that they rise to the occasion, build an administrative will and by giving leadership to the bureaucracy work for the teeming millions masses of India and for giving fillip to the economic development of the country. As there is no alternative to the bureaucratic government in democracy, one can only hope that good sense will prevail among the bureaucrats to look after the interest of the nation and its people.

REFERENCES

1. "Commonwealth Secretariat: A Profile of the Public Service of India", Commonwealth Secretariat, Marlborough House, Pall Mall, London, 2004, p 13.
2. Dhar, TN, "Indian Administrative Service in Uttar Pradesh: Perspectives – Past and Present", in *Governance and the IAS*, Dar, RK (ed), Tata McGraw-Hill Publishing Company, New Delhi, 1999, pp 320-21.
3. Ibid, pp 323-26.
4. Ibid, p 327.
5. Ibid, p 256.
6. Ibid, p 296.
7. Ibid, p 260.

3

Institution of Ombudsman to Prevent Misuse of Bureaucratic Authority

Ombudsman is a dynamic institution for achieving administrative justice. No institution can live long unless it is founded on just and fair principles. Ombudsman provides accessible and inexpensive assistance in ensuring rights to the individual citizen or group of citizens to just and fair treatment by and service from the State and its agencies. Being human, administrators and public decision-makers make mistakes. Secondly, the public service is on a higher pedestal in developing and undeveloped countries. This position is exploited by the bureaucrats. Therefore, it is germane to make good the wrongs done to the citizens by the authoritative bureaucrats specially in cases of the disadvantaged and vulnerable sections of the society.

Earlier Ombudsman institution was confined to the Scandinavia. Now the office is a global phenomenon estimated to be operative in about ninety countries. It has become necessary evil. A democratic government is run only through the bureaucrats. But bureaucratic power, if it is not properly controlled, is itself destructive of democracy and its values. Ombudsman is an insurance against the bureaucratic arrogance, nepotism, corruption and is a citizens' protector. The Swedish word Ombudsman means someone who acts on behalf of another and takes up his or her problems with government and public authorities generally.

Ombudsman was appointed in 1809 in Sweden, Finland in 1999, Denmark in 1955, Norway in 1962 and New Zealand in 1962. In the course of next three decades, the office multiplied rapidly, at the national, regional and municipal levels of government, spreading throughout the liberal democracies of Western Europe, North America, the Caribbean, Australia and the Pacific region, and reached parts of the Middle-East, Africa and the Indian subcontinent.

Ombudsman – A Reality

In democracies, the government changes by the people's change of mind. The new set of political executives come on the plank or issues like removing of corruption and providing transparent and expeditious government action. Therefore, bureaucrats cannot prevent Ombudsman from being placed in the polity. Secondly, at one stage, the subordinate bureaucrats don't follow the discipline. Therefore, at one point of time, it becomes indispensable to bring in Ombudsman to run even the bureaucratic organizations. Therefore, persons working in the public service have to mentally accept its existence and co-operate with Ombudsman. The United Nations Convention Against Corruption also enjoins upon nations to ensure clean and responsive governance to their citizens and to establish effective bodies to contain and punish acts of corruption and to provide for prompt and fair investigation and prosecution in cases of corruption. Thus, the public officials and staff have to re-orient themselves and convince their families that there will be no extra income through corruption in their government jobs. If they indulge in it, they will have to be prepared to be persecuted, forgo promotion and to go to jails if they are found guilty for unfair practices not warranted by law. I am sure that this new approach though a sour pill, yet is a pill which the most powerful bureaucrats cannot escape. The awareness among citizens now at a very high level which was demonstrated in the year 2013 in India when the whole nation demanded establishment of Lokpal at the Central Government's level and the government was overturned *inter alia* on this issue in 2014 General Elections in India.

Types of Ombudsman

At present, there are six types of Ombudsman:

(i) The Ombudsman is for general purpose for all complaints across the whole spectrum of governmental action and activities at all levels of government;

(ii) A special purpose or dedicated Ombudsman who is concerned with one area of administration such as health, environment, police force or for needs of particular groups such as ethnic minorities, indigenous people, the disabled or children;

(iii) Ombudsman at the international or supra-national level of governance like in the World Bank, the IMF,

WHO regarding the staff complaints in international organizations;

(iv) A Human Rights Ombudsman, Civil Rights Ombudsman or hybrid offices;

(v) In-house complaints redressal Ombudsman in government department and government agencies.

(vi) Private Sector Ombudsman offering protection for the consumers in the fields of commerce and industry like Banking Ombudsman in India, Australia, New Zealand, Singapore etc.

"As an alternative to the courts or the activities of elected representatives the Ombudsman institution clearly has its attractions. There is likely to be a large and increasingly important role for it, in dealing with both injustice caused by bad administration in general and the denial of social, economic and cultural rights in particular. Practical improvements in administration are best achieved by the unearthing, non confrontational and cooperative approach adopted by Ombudsmen, who tend to rely as much as possible on conciliation and persuasion, with the aim of achieving solutions and settlements."[1]

The Ombudsman Scene in India

The provinces/States in federal India have gone ahead of Centre to establish in the Ombudsman known as the Lokayukta. The office of Lokayukta exists in Maharashtra (1971), Bihar (1973), Rajasthan (1973), Uttar Pradesh (1975), Madhya Pradesh (1981), Andhra Pradesh (1983), Himachal Pradesh (1983), Karnataka (1985), Assam (1986) etc. Odisha was the first State to pass Ombudsman legislation in 1970 and also the first to abolish the institution in 1993.

The Lokayukta has powers to make investigations in regard to all administrative actions form the level of Ministers to the lower levels including Chairman, Zila Parishad (District Council) and other local bodies. The 'Grievances' in addition to allegations have been covered under the legislations of Maharashtra, Bihar, Uttar Pradesh, Karnataka, Assam and Kerala. Other States have incorporated only 'allegation'. Madhya Pradesh Lokayukta is very effective as the Special Police Establishment is placed directly under him free from influence of the executive. Therefore, MP Lokayukta is always in news. It raids many public servants and seizes their properties worth millions of rupees disproportionate to their known sources of Income. In UP many corrupt ministers have been caught and are languishing in jails because at the time of permission by the Chief Minister, their political opponents are in government. To give just an idea of work load of some of the Lokayuktas, the number of cases received and disposed of during year 1993 are given below:

States	Complaints Received	Complaints Disposed Off
Andhra Pradesh	3,180	2,329
Assam	188	105
Bihar	3,156	2,278
Himachal Pradesh	27	10
Karnataka	2,129	1,174
Madhya Pradesh	4,082 (Only 892 were registered)	786
Maharashtra	9,038	8,942[2]

The Lokayuktas of Madhya Pradesh and Andhra Pradesh have achieved greater success than other States. In general, the Lokayukta scheme has been regarded more as a failure in dealing with corruption cases. However, the organization has over the years, successfully provided relief to a number of complainants concerning grievance cases arising out of mal administration.

Lokpal and Lokayuktas Act 2013 and Aftermath

To deal with corruption among public functionaries, the new Act, the Lokpal and Lokayuktas Act, 2013 has been brought into effect on public demand, and protests led by the public activist Shri Anna Hazare.

According to the Act, the Lokpal will be a multi member body. Its jurisdiction extends to Prime Minister, Minister of the Union, Member of Parliament and all government employees of A, B, C and D groups *viz* from the peon to the Secretary of the Department or from the constable to the Prime Minister of India under Section 14(h), the NGOs, societies or trusts are also included within the fold of the definition under the Act.

The Lokpal will conduct preliminary inquiry and can refer the matter for inquiry and investigation to Central Bureau of Investigation or to Central Vigilance Commission in respect of Central Government employees of all categories. After the report is received, it will give opportunity for hearing to the public servant and will then decide whether to proceed further or close the matter. Preliminary inquiry is to be conducted within maximum 90 days and investigation by CBI within one year at the most. The Lokpal will then decide after obtaining the comments of the competent authority and the public servant whether to order for prosecution or departmental proceedings. Competent authority is prescribed under Section 2(c) of the Act which is generally Minister incharge of the Ministry or Department in case of an officer. The Selection Committee will have Prime Minister as Chairperson and Chief Justice of India or a Judge of the Supreme Court nominated by him apart from Speaker of Lok Sabha, Leader of Opposition and an eminent jurist.

The Lokpal has the power of superintendence over CVC and CBI, and can give direction to them in respect of matters referred by him. The Lokpal can also order for search and seizure of documents. Lokpal can order provisional attachment for the period for not more than ninety days. The Special Court may confirm such attachment or not. Where Special Court has reason to believe or is satisfied that the assets, proceeds, receipts and benefits have arisen or procured by means of corruption by the public servants, it may authorize the confiscation of such assets etc till his acquittal. The Central Government will have to constitute number of special courts as the Lokpal may recommend and the special courts shall ensure completion of each trial within a period of one year. The Special Court can also assess the loss caused by the action or decisions of the public servant pursuant to a conspiracy with the beneficiary, such loss may also be recovered from such beneficiary proportionately. This is a provision in Section 44 of the Act that every public servant shall make a declaration of his assets and of his spouses and liabilities every year before 31st July as on 31st March each year. After seven years from the date of offence, no complaint will be entertained by the Lokpal. The complaints and their disposal will be displayed on website of Lokpal.

The mandatory provision has been added in Section 63, Part III of the Act that State Legislature will establish the body of Lokayukta to deal with complaints of corruption against certain public functionaries within a period of one year. Time will tell how this new institution codified as Ombudsman in India will function.

> "Where corruption is rampant, and where nepotism has infiltrated right from the Ministerial level to lower officials, it is highly doubtful if a Lokpal can produce any notable as well as appreciable improvement in administration. Unless and until we provide a basically sound, healthy society, no good result should be expected from the proposed reform. The institution is nevertheless worth a trial."[3]

Need of Administrative Law for India

The Indians prefer codified law. Most of the bureaucrats do not know the applicable law, rules and notifications in their dealings.

In India, the consciousness about law or knowledge of law has not informed all the bureaucrats of the country though this is the first prerequisite of any law of the land. Though setting up of administrative bodies and separate administrative courts to adjudicate matters will involve lot of expenditure, yet it will be worthwhile if statutory administrative law is enforced in the country, which will also function as code of conduct for the public officers and employees. The power of the administration is to act suo motu and to impose directly on the subject the duty to obey its decisions. But the power is to be exercised within the ambit of law, which protects individuals against administrative arbitrariness.

The Supreme Court in some cases have struck down purely administrative actions and even fined the top executives like the Union Minister for the cases of arbitrary allotment of petrol pumps and Central Government quarters in Delhi. The Supreme Court has even reviewed appointments on the top administrative posts in Govt. of India and in some State Governments. By these decisions, the Supreme Court has won the popularity of the masses. On the other hand, the administrative system is becoming gradually indecisive and inactive. The senior officers are always afraid of review of their actions or decisions by the High Courts or the Supreme Court. The sword of Contempt of Court always hangs on their neck. In such an environment, a permanent Civil Service who are the decision makers, will not like to fiddle with their careers. As a result, the economic and social developments will come to standstill gradually.

Let us analyse, how this problem can be solved and a healthy balance struck so that administrative actions or decisions become not only just and fair but also speedy. Lack of speed is the only cause why India is still in the comity of developing nations. The senior civil officers are left alone to face courts when there are cases of Contempt of Court against them. Actually, the subordinates down the line have no sense of proportion or judicial bent of mind to put up the notes, suggestions or drafts before them so that they can speedily take just and fair decisions.

The solutions are manifold. Some will suggest that there should be proper recruitment methods. Second school of thought will suggest for extensive training, retraining and continuous training up to the clerk level in the bureaucracy for human resource development. This is not feasible at present because training itself will involve a huge expenditure and development of large infrastructures. The simplest solution is to have an 'Administrative Law' for India.

Apart from body of law, the administrative law should also contain general code of conduct, which will be generally and equally applicable to all members of the public bureaucracy irrespective of their rank or position in the government. This code of conduct will also help to cover unforeseen situations, actions in unforeseen or emergency situations, commissions or omission by the bureaucrat.

> "This whole body of law, rules and guidelines will help the members of public bureaucracy to enlighten themselves regarding their rights, duties and decision-making process in the bureaucratic organization which is intricately linked with the progress of the society or the nation. They will treat it like their Ramayana or the Bible. Thus, the chances of their *bona fide* errors in decision-making will be less. Many of the cases will not go to law courts delaying the matters further for decision. Last but not the least, public will be greatly benefited by the just and fair decision making process at various levels of the bureaucracy and will place their faith and trust in the government bureaucracy."[4]

Concluding Remarks

It is now well recognized world over that on one hand, the State should have institution of Ombudsman to tame and keep bureaucrats in check. At the same time, the bureaucrats should have proper knowledge, training or code of ethics or conduct rules for them so that they may not falter. After all, no government can run smoothly without their willing co-operation as bureaucracy is the base of the State and is a strong organization with lot of unity in its working and its accountability.

REFERENCES

1. Gregory, Roy and Giddings, Philip (eds), *Righting Wrongs: The Ombudsman in Six Continents*, IOS Press, Amsterdam (The Netherlands), 2000, pp 16 and 17.
2. Jha, Rajani Ranjan, "The Ombudsman Scene in India", Ibid, p 260.
3. Kesari, UPD, *Lectures on Administrative Law*, Central Law Agency, Allahabad, 1972, p 141.
4. Agrawal, Dr PK, "Need of Administrative Law for India", in *I am Sorry: Indian Bureaucracy at Crossroads*, Dr PK Agrawal and N Vittal (eds), Manas Publications, New Delhi, 2008, pp 187, 189 and 197.

4

Values of the American Bureaucrats

The public bureaucracy is like the proverbial elephant in a living room which in spite of its detractors, is alive, well, proliferating and hybridizing. It is not very monolithic as the Weberian public bureaucracy but is multiple. "It is a many-sided, evolving, diversified organization device. The British bureaucrats are *inter alia* something of an expert in the ways of the constitution, a bit of a politician, a stickler for procedure and a stoic able to accept disappointments with equanimity.[1] The bureaucracy or bureaucrats in America have historically contributed to the efficiency and effectiveness to the entire process of governance keeping pace with the time. The bureaucrats have thus integrated their values to support and develop responsible governance for the liberty loving Americans, the bureaucracy has become a condition of freedom specially in view of the recent upsurge of corporate scandals in the United States.

Virtually every aspect of daily lives in US is regulated to some degree by one or the other of the numerous administrative agencies that make up the national bureaucracy of America. The powers of these agencies are extensive, being judicial and legislature in nature as well as executive. The Constitution of United States of America states that these fundamental powers of government should be separated into three branches that have effective checks and balances in relation to each other. Otherwise, arbitrary government will prevail.

The system of governance in USA still conforms to principle of *laissez-faire* ie for forms of government let fools contest whatever is least administered is best. Most of the Americans tend to agree with this Parkinson's Law and this is practically followed in US because there is exorbitant rise in private business and industries that government functions have been cornered.

Nature of the American Bureaucracy

The American administrative agencies, to survive, need political support of Congress. Congress controls finances and has ultimate power over re-organization.

> "The activity of bureaucrats within organizations also reveals the political nature of bureaucracy. Though these bureaucrats are assigned formal roles, such roles are frequently and easily short-circuited by those attempting to maintain, solidify, or expand their positions, in the same way that the organization as a whole plays a political game to advance its own interest."[2]

> "The President of USA is a very powerful head of State. Therefore, he controls the bureaucracy rather the bureaucracy controls him as in many other small countries. However, there is separation of power in America at all levels to divide and arrange the several offices in such a manner, that each may be a check on the other;

> that the private interest of every individual, may be sentinel over the public rights."[3]

There is always a need to control the abuses of government. If men were angels, no government would be necessary. If angels were to govern man, neither external nor internal controls on government would be necessary. In framing a government, which is to be administered by men over men, the great difficulty lies in this. You must first enable the government to control the governed; and in the next place, oblige it to control itself.

On the one hand governments were faced with a demand for new controls over the private economic sphere, and on the other they were pressured by very powerful and wealthy groups to maintain *laissez-faire*. The net result was the establishment of limited government control of the economy. Similarly, it was felt necessary to make bureaucratic organization as democratic one as administrative constituencies are compared of diverse groups with divergent attitudes.

Since the New Deal

A virtual abdication of congressional power to the President and the administrative power was brought about by the World War II: Extraordinary delegations were made and upheld by the courts, and it was during this period that the substitution of administrative for congressional standards was allowed. President Roosevelt was a very assertive President. He didn't like various branches taking decisions even like ship-building without his approval. The President only came to know through the *New York Times*. The Constitution doesn't enable the President to exercise controlling power over the bureaucracy.

But regardless of the separation of powers, the Presidency in USA is the focal point of leadership in the American system. The President stands at the centre of an extra-ordinary complex and diverse system of government, and he, as all politicians and agencies, must strive to maintain a balance of political support in his favour.

The primary legal checks upon presidential power over the bureaucracy come from statutes which determine basic organizational patterns. Statutes may limit the President's control over particular spheres of activity by assigning sole responsibility for action to an administrative agency or officer. Moreover, Congress frequently gives independent authority to subordinate bureaus within executive departments. With such legal authority as a starting point, a stubborn official can defy the wishes of the President again and again. Unless the President wants to make an issue of such defiance and as a last resort, ask the official to resign, there is little he can do. Roosevelt's New Deal policy was to have committed bureaucrats around. However, gradually it got diluted and got converted into merit system and career bureaucrats like in India became more in positions because their mandate was to take the economic system ahead. But conflict among the administrative agencies like during World War II known as 'battle of Washington' also surfaces here and there.

The merit system is not the only legal obstacle faced by the President with respect to the appointment and removal powers. When Congress provides that administrative positions shall be filled by Presidential appointments, the confirmation of the Senate is usually required. And, of course, the Constitution requires Senatorial confirmation of presidential appointments of ambassadors, "other public ministers and consultants," and judges of the Supreme Court. The President's Cabinet must be confirmed by the Senate, and although it is generally a formality, from time to time the Senate refuses to accept the President's choice; for example, at the end of Eisenhower's second term, the Senate turned down the appointment of Lewis Strauss, an experienced but controversial public servant, to become Secretary of Commerce. He had formerly been Chairman of the Atomic Energy Commission during the Eisenhower administration. President Kennedy proposed similar changes to increase Presidential Power over the agencies, and again most of his recommendations were rejected although he managed to increase the power of the Chairmen of some agencies, such as the Federal Trade Commission. The trend is in giving greater control to the President through these appointments.

The agencies are given freedom within their spheres of activity by the President and his staff unless the interests of the White House are directly affected.

> "The American Presidency is a great institution, but the President is not in fact Chief Administrator. He cannot, nor does he wish to, control all the complex activities engaged in by the administrative branch. In many key areas of Presidential responsibility, he demands, and generally receives, loyalty from administrative agencies. But in other fields the agencies function with partial autonomy the policy spheres that have been assigned to them by Congress."[4]

> "But this growth of bureaucracy is not a cause of alarm. It adds an important new dimension to our government. American bureaucracy takes its place as an equal partner with the President, Congress, and the Judiciary. Its existence not only increases the ability of our

> government to meet the challenges of the twentieth century, but also enhances the meaning of constitutional democracy."[5]

It transpires that so far the American bureaucrat is functioning with his powers vested on him/her by the statute and is impartial and honest, the President cannot question his functioning or he cannot be removed from his position. As there is transparency to a large extent in functioning of the bureaucracy in USA, the bureaucrats have lot of autonomy, peace of mind and independence in their working. These values have stabilized in bureaucracy of US after lot of experience of history.

The Watergate and Enron scandals gave a jolt to the American system to rethink and to rebuild the bureaucracy or public management not around the politicians in 'spoils system' but to make it immune from political upheavals so that it has not to change after the change of President. As a result, it takes time for the bureaucracy to re-orient itself. Some of the instances gave this idea to take deep roots which are enumerated as below.

1. Enron's Failure

Enron's executives were not too concerned about the laws. Enron and Ogilvy decided to have its vision, and its new ad campaign, around a concept called "what we believe". Those belief included the wisdom of 'open market' and being a 'laboratory for innovation'. This was corporate equivalent to moralist libertarianism. They circumvented energy market regulations and accounting laws. This annoyed State bureaucracy and the Enron's top management were jailed for offences committed and the corporation went into liquidation. It was established that Enron's officials had bribed the Indian politicians to set up a naphtha plant for power generation in Maharashtra province, India and had manipulated accounts to deceive the audit. Resultantly the company's auditors PWC were also held guilty by the bureaucracy to manipulate accounts of Enron Incorporation.

2. Watergate Scandal

The Watergate scandal was a major political scandal that occurred in the US in the 1970s and the Nixon administration attempted cover up of its involvement. It included bugging up the offices of political opponents DNC headquaters at Watergate offices in Washington DC and other suspicious people. As a result of proved misuse of powers, President Nixon resigned on August 9, 1974. The scandal also resulted in the indictment of 69 people, out of whom 48 were found guilty, many of whom were Nixon's top administrative officials.

President Nixon first refused to hand over recorded tapes. On the order, he handed over the tapes which proved his involvement. Facing near certain impeachment in the House of Representatives, he resigned which is the only incident so far in the American history.

3. Failure of CIA in Iraq

CIA had misguided that Iraq had weapons of mass destruction and there was an imminent threat. However, no such evidence was found after USA and UK succeeded in change of regime in Iraq after removing Saddam Hussein. Later on, it was instructed that analytical processes at CIA should be further improved to avoid this kind of error in the future.

4. Clinton-Monica Lewinsky Affair

President Bill Clinton was having intimate relation with one of his intern Monica Lewinsky at the White House. His flirtation with the young lady made a laughing stock in USA. However, on enquiry, the sex scandal couldn't be proved against Clinton and was more or less consensual amorous play. Had it been proved as sex exploitation of his employee, the most powerful public servant of USA had to resign. In moralistic countries like India, it is sufficient for a highly placed person to at least resign. Thus, USA believes in equality at work-place for men and women.

5. Success Story of World Trade Center Mishap

Minutes after the first plane hit the World Trade Center (WTC) in Manhattan on the morning of September 11, 2001, the Director of Emergency Management for New York City activated an Emergency Operation Center on the 23rd Floor of WTC. There, without consulting the Mayor, he closed all streets below canal, as well as all tunnels and bridges around Manhattan. Suddenly his centre's offices were hit by flying debris, so the director moved the emergency command centre to a WTC lobby. From there he arranged for the Coast Guard to seal New York's harbours and the Defence Department to block its city's air space. The Transportation Commissioner rerouted buses and ferries to remove people from Manhattan. The director and train master of the commuter train to New Jersey, standing on the concourse beneath the WTC, ordered a loading incoming train to skip the WTC stop and return to New Jersey. In the opening hours of this tragic day upwards of 3,000 people were safely removed from the scene of this historic disaster.

Public Participation: New Innovations

> "For many years bureau have employed a variety of institutional techniques to engage the public directly in their planning, management, operations, and decision making activities. These include advisory groups, citizen boards, town meetings, neighbourhood meetings, community workshops, community score cards, focus groups, planning forms, citizen policy panels, agenda formation exercises, citizen coordinating councils and volunteer activities."[6]

In spite of performing all kinds of activities at the behest of his political master, the bureaucrat can not detach himself from political administration from 'personal' ideals and loyalties.

Today, the US is an attractive option for anyone who is seeking a career opportunity even in US bureaucracy. There are many outsiders including the Indians who are on top slots in the American bureaucracy. Most of the cities in USA are cosmopolitan globally and it reflects that the US bureaucracy gives due regard to merit unlike in other countries. This is one of the norms why US economy is world's largest economy and USA is the most powerful country in the world.

According to Weber (1978; 958 off) the bureau comprises the social and cultural conditions of a distinctive and independent compartments of the person, one that is basically non-sectarian in character. For Weber, the ethical attributes of the good bureaucrat –

> "strict adherence to procedure, acceptance of sub- and super-ordination, *esprit de corps*, abnegation of personal moral enthusiasm, commitment to the purposes of the office – are to be seen as a positive moral achievement requiring the mastery of definite ethical techniques and realities declaring one's 'personal'

> interest, developing appropriate professional relations with one's colleagues, subordinating one's 'self' to the dictates of procedural decision-making – through which individuals come to acquire the disposition and ability to conduct themselves according to the ethos of bureaucratic office."[7]

Thus, the American bureaucrat is in a dilemma whether to conform to the instructions of the boss urgently or leave it to be decided by the expert panel. Bending has no limit. If the senior civil servants favour the political executives in respect of their policies and personal or party interests, the street level bureaucrat might use her discretion to 'bend the rules' in favour of an individual citizen.

These street level bureaucrats have proved problems for the great institution bureaucracy around the world including USA. The public has direct contact with them and formulate its opinion based on this lower level interaction. The citizens hardly find smooth avenues to complain against these street levels bureaucrats who are called inspectors in India.

> "As it is difficult to streamline street level bureaucrats, it is argued in USA, that the State can no longer assume a monopoly of either expertise or of the resources necessary to govern but must rely on a plurality or interdependent institutions and actors drawn from within and beyond government. Government is engaged in co-regulation, co-steering, co-production, co-operative management, public-private partnerships and other forms of governing that cross the boundaries between government and society as well as between public and private sectors."[8]

Thus economy and efficiency are two great challenges before the American bureaucracy. In USA, the bureaucrats may draw higher salaries, but they are not allowed access to the kind of capital, a private company employee is allowed. Secondly, in US bureaucracy a proper gender ratio is to be maintained which is balanced in most of the jobs but females are more employed in lower jobs.

Concluding Remarks

In view of corporate globalization, conceptions of public interest, public good and public services are changing. It is to fulfil aspiration of all by raising standards of living. The public feel that public institutions and bureaucrats are driven by venal, self-interested and self-seeking motivations (just like markets), rather than altruism, public service goals, or professional ethics. The new forms of public service delivery pose new problems of controls and co-ordination. There is desire for high quality public service with doubts about the capacity of government to provide them.

> "The public expect governments to perform like governments – fulfilling promises, meeting demands, and improving standards while being increasingly sceptical about their claims to have done so. These conditions constitute the possibilities for the rise of 'performance' as a governmental and a political project."[9]

The politicians dance at the wing of the public to win votes and to continue in power. Therefore, life of a bureaucrat in USA and other countries is going to be very tough. They can no longer sit on their laurels under the king's shelter as the king has given away their powers to the public in democracy. Their perquisites and privileges are going to be curtailed drastically and they will be more accountable to the public day-by-day in view of transparency through media, social media and right to information vested in public in popular democracies in the world including USA.

The public like to see them beyond an iota of doubt as regards their integrity. The public like to see them working more efficiently than the private sector. At the same time, they will continue to be paid lower compensation than their counterpart in the private sector. The bureaucrats can be held liable and accountable as regards various schemes of their departments and can be asked to pay fine for intentional delays and indecisions.

Thus, there is growing realization among public that public servants or bureaucrats must be more efficient, honest and sincere so that mission for the welfare of the last man in the society is achieved by the bureaucrat.[9]

REFERENCES

1. Gay, Paul du, *The Values of Bureaucracy*, Oxford University Press, Oxford, 2005, p 4.
2. Woll, Peter, *American Bureaucracy*, WW Norton & Company, New York (USA), 1963, p 5.
3. Ibid, Madison, Federalists, p 19.
4. Ibid, p 173.
5. Ibid, p 177.
6. Ibid, p 33.
7. Ibid, p 52.
8. Ibid, p 193.
9. Ibid, p 215.

5

Motivation and Bureaucrats

Motivation is an individual problem but an organization cannot afford to create all such innumerable work situations and thus, they have to adopt a common strategy for the motivation of its employees. Employees come from diverse educational, ethnic and socio-economic backgrounds. There is difference in individual's perception and behaviour. We must also understand why one employee works at less than 50% of standard and another works at over 150% of standard.

Motivation Defined

Motivation literally means incentive. It is concerned with the initiation of action. It is an incitement of the will. It is a consideration or emotion that excites to action. Interestingly saying, it is the power in an engine to move.

Motivation is something that moves the person to action, and continues him in the course of action already initiated. Therefore, maintaining a person in work is also a part of motivation. Without that, motivation will not contribute much for the well-being of the organization. Motivation in an organization is the willingness of an employee to respond to organizational requirements.

Motivational Tools

Following factors can be summarized to motivate the employees:

(i) A well-defined humanistic personnel policy wherein the work-force is regarded as the valuable assets of the organization.

(ii) Fairness in recruitment and selection, placement of the right job, sound and fair promotion and transfer policies and need-based training and development programmes.

(iii) Fair wages and salary administration ensuring equitable wage structure free from internal and external inequalities.

(iv) Reward for good performance and punishment to the lazy and the crooks.

(v) A constructive and objective system of performance appraisal and assessment rating of employees.

(vi) Prompt handling of worker's grievances.

(vii) In handling disciplinary cases, the management should not only be fair but should also seem to be fair.

(viii) Participative management.

(ix) Job enrichment and enlargement.

(x) Self example, the dictum: "before you motivate others, you must first motivate yourself."

The following negative factors should also be taken care of which demotivate or demoralize the employees.

(i) Under assignment.

(ii) Over assignment.

(iii) Buck mastership ie the superiors or leaders are finding fault with the subordinates which may erode employee's motivation.

The motivation as a tool has to be carefully scrutinized and used. The motivation as a psychological factor can be further analysed and concretized under the following constituents.

System of Macro Environment

An organization cannot function in a vacuum. It is a part of social system. An organization is a combination of two systems, the technology, the tasks, the equipment and working arrangements, the inter-personal relationship of employees and the social system. The two systems are in constant interaction and each influences the other. An organization in a war-torn country will find its working interrupted. Strikes in work, in society, public transport, municipal services do effect working of individuals.

Thus, macro elements are very essential to constitute motivation. The workers in Japan and Germany worked relentlessly after the ravage of the two countries after their defeat in the Second World War because the employees were motivated by the idea of patriotism. The main input in Japan was importation of Taylor's Scientific Management which began around 1920. The industrial engineer begins to work with people who have to do the job long before he finishes his analysis. He will use the work-force as his resource when he has finished his analysis. The synthesis will essentially be done by the work-group itself. Thus, the Japanese worker very largely takes responsibility for improving his tools.

There are no barriers in supervisory officers and staff. All share the open desks and chairs under the same roof and join the same clubs in the night together. This co-operation in all works of life has made the Japanese system very conducive for work output. Even then Japanese management can hardly be accused of having abdicated. They have more authority than management as in the West. In USA there is divine right of the management as, the last word known as management prerogative. But the prerogative is exercised quite democratically and judiciously. The Managers have learnt there that decentralization strengthens the top management. It results in greater authority for top management which can concentrate on more important tasks.

In socialistic system, the management is based on full public participation and more by personal example. For example, Fidel Castro, the President of Cuba himself worked in sugarcane field and the results were equitably distributed among all.

In India, the management has no definite philosophy. It suffers from British legacy of feudalism i e excessive love for rules and procedures and secondly they cannot exercise their prerogative properly because of lack of their will-power, confidence or political interference.

Financial Incentives

If the workers are worried about their salaries, housing safety and security, much energy will be wasted in their efforts to ensure these things. If the manager cannot help in these matters, he can at least, be sympathetic to workers and do the little he can do within his capacity. In USA, financial incentives, or compensation is the most important factor whereas it is not so in countries like Japan and India

At present, monthly workers feel deficit as regards financial side. This is largely because of their high standard of living and high expectations which cannot probably be met by the organization. But financial incentive should be enough to keep a reasonable persons (not spendthrift) in mental balance to work. Therefore, such conditions should be created.

Personnel Management

A climate for interdependence rather than dependency should be created. A team spirit should be created. Rewards and punishments should go side by side. Rewards may not always be in financial terms. Even a word of appreciation has great motivating value.

A good manager should also motivate his worker through guidance and counselling.

On the other hand, there should be well laid down personnel policy, within knowledge of all the employees. There should be proper performance appraisal system and promotion etc based only on objective consideration. There should be no partiality. There should be a well-defined and active employees' grievance-handling machinery. There should be a scope for comparison with other organizations and there should be provided an inherent mechanism to make least required corrections or improvement.

Job Enrichment

Harzberg describes job enrichment as that type of improvement in the context of the job which may give a worker more of a challenge, more of a complete task, more responsibility, more opportunity for growth and more challenge to continue his ideas. This will solve the problem of increasing alienation of workers from their jobs in creating a serious human relation problem. Job enlargement may also help. Job enrichment provides the opportunity for the employee's psychological growth. The job enrichment will thus include:

(i) Rotation of tasks;
(ii) Increasing responsibilities;
(iii) Variety of methods;
(iv) Reducing task specialization to make a complete natural unit;
(v) Removing controls;
(vi) Participation of employees;
(vii) Introducing reward for more difficult tasks.

This will result in fullness of work, high quality work performance, low absenteeism and high turnover and high motivation with the work.

A recent survey of 58 companies with job enrichment programme has revealed that two-thirds felt that product quality had improved and half said that employee turnover was down to an average of 18%.

Leadership

Leadership is the capacity to frame plans which will succeed and the faculty to persuade others to carry them out in the face of all difficulties. Therefore, leadership is something which can create motivation without any resource because a leader has the greatest quality to tackle people. A leader has the capacity to give reward, can exercise coercive power, is an expert and has referent ability. They know the art to utilize the people who are the greatest resource of assets. Top management as leader of the organization is the directing, vision-setting, standard-setting organ. He treats people as resource to himself.

Dr Thomas Holmes found that out of 150 points, boss contributes 23-point psychological problem that results in physical illness. If one talks to an employee, he will always talk about his boss. Therefore, to improve the work-culture, it is prerequisite that the bosses ie leaders should improve themselves first, because 17% tension may be contributed by them. They should be pragmatic, forward-looking, humans and should be able to put themselves into the shoes of the employees. An ideal leader should have an ideal vision or knowledge of handling people and of the job or self. He should have courage to decide. He should have will power to persist to his task. He should have initiated to be a self-starter.

In the Indian Army's credo, the safety, honour and welfare of the country comes first and self case, comfort or safety comes last for army man. In such exceptional situation, the leadership plays the main role and calculations of personnel management for performance appraisals are defeated.

In the Indian context, a leader should have a good grasp and pride in the long history, constitutional idealism of secularism and cultural ethos of India. In India, personality cut still rules supreme. Therefore, it is only good leader who can inculcate following tools of motivation in the organization.

(a) He can motivate individually through guidance and counselling. He has to interact with different workers who have different need patterns. He may encounter very efficient workers, poor workers, problem creators and all kinds of individuals.

(b) A competitive climate can be created through recognition of good work. Recognition and public acknowledgment help workers to value their work deriving a sense of satisfaction and feeling of importance from it. This goes a long way in motivating the workers if rewarding is impartial. They work harder and have a sense of competition among them.

(c) Creation of a climate of problem solving rather than avoidance is a must. The good manager faces issues and constantly struggles to overcome them. Approach-oriented managers do well because their workers also develop, this style of facing problems. Managers should attempt to encourage their workers to be problem-solvers rather than avoiders. A manager who cannot take responsibility himself also cannot let his subordinates take responsibility.

(d) Creation of a productive climate through personal example is required. Workers are constantly looking to their boss to set an example. They tend to imitate him and his style may, percolate down the hierarchy. If he is authoritarian and non-trusting, his next level workers may attempt to be like him too, ultimately creating a climate of suspicion in the organization.

Now a days, the workers have become very conscious. They would not listen or obey to a leader who preaches something but practices a different thing. Therefore, personal example has become the most important factor in the present day scenario of motivation in the field of management.

Relative Significance of Factors

For giving inter priority or significance, we may conclude that macro environment will contribute 12% of the motivation as because employees like in Japan, Germany and Russia after the Second World War defied all facts in work place and worked for the country by rendering high degree of production or service.

The financial or material incentive will occupy, one fourth part of motivation. The importance of salary as motivating factor is not realized unless there is a break or stoppage in periodic achievements due to financial shortage or some other problem. All work gets stopped at once. Most of the municipal bodies suffer from dilemma and are in the vicious circle of non-payment of financial incentives.

The personnel management factors like promotion policies, job evaluation and monitoring, review or appraisal will also carry 25% weight to the total scenario of motivation at least in the Indian context.

Job enrichment factors should be attached 13% significance as they provide a variety which is a psychological sauce of the employees. A Chowkidar standing guard for whole of his life, finds out ways to choose path of least duty or resistance. How can a clerk of a business enterprise enjoy doing accounting for all his life? The job of the policemen also seems monotonous unless there is a rotation. Inter-departmental or sectional transfers in an industrial undertaking will provide freshness and fresh outlook to an otherwise boring employees. Twenty-five percent significance may be attached to the quality of leadership. Based on above, the extent of motivation will be arrived by concretizing a term which is emotional, psychological, inner urge or of behavioural dynamics.

Formula devised:

The variable as discussed thus is:

(i) System ie micro-environment.
(ii) System ie macro environment.
(iii) Financial incentives.
(iv) Personnel Management.
(v) Job enrichment
(vi) Leadership

These variables can be expressed in terms of linear equation as follows:

$$M = S_1E + S_2I + S_3P + S_4J + S_5L \ldots S_nF_n{}^1$$

Where M is the total or resultant motivation.

S_1 is the weightage or ranking of the factor.

E, I, P, J, L represent various factors such as environment, financial incentives, personnel matters, job enrichment and leadership. We can also denote them as:

$$M = S_1F_1 + S_2F_2 + S_3F_3 \ldots S_nF_n$$

i e
$$M\ (T) = \sum_{I=0}^{I=10} S_1F_1$$

In order to implement above equation, it is necessary to fix the weightage factor S_1, S_2, S_3, S_4, S_5 or any other coefficient or factor taken later on. The weightage *inter-se* was already determined based on the concept or decisions of the research. Here, one cannot avoid subjectively. Thus, the facts were given following weightage:

$$F_1 = E = 12\% = 12S_1$$
$$F_2 = (\text{Financial}) = 25\% = 25S_2$$
$$F_3 = P = 25\% = 25S_3$$
$$F_4 = J = 13\% = 13S_4$$
$$F_5 = L = 25\% = 25S_5$$

To reduce subjectively in measurement of strength of a factor, help of Likert scale may be taken which is also used for measurement of psychological factors like attitude which is a kin to motivation. Likert Scale is also called 'summated ratings scale'. Let us construct the following five statements or decisions relating to issues under investigation as follows:

Very High	assigned	10 marks
High	assigned	6 marks
Average	assigned	5 marks
Low	assigned	2 marks
Very low	assigned	0 marks

Using this method of scoring, total scoring is calculated depending on the strength of each factor.

In case of ideal situation, all S_i will get 10 ranking points. The coefficients in the factor equations are called 'factor loadings'. The equation may be depicted in a random case as

$$M(T) = 10F_1 + 8F_2 + 5F_3 + 2F_4 + 0F_5^2$$

Where, F_i are already fixed by way of survey, analysis interpretation of good experience and reasoning.

Thus, the whole purpose of this exercise is to concretise the idea that the motivation, though a vague human psychological term, may be fitted in a mathematical jacket or formula so that it may not be arbitrarily subjected to whims or fancies of individual evaluator.

The above equation will thus, be reduced in purely numerical form. However, there are two cautions before arriving at the total motivation of basis of five motivational tools in an organization.

(i) All other factors responsible for motivation or demotivation should also be brought within one of the nearer defined factors.

(ii) Weightage factors may be determined after careful scrutiny and discussions.

Let us now examine how a scientific approach to psychology can be adopted and how the above additive empirical formula for motivation well compares or suits with other measurement devices in the realm of motivation especially in a work place environment.

> "The strength of attitude is a measure of the strength of a course of action, or tendency to a course of action, in response to stimulii. They have calculated based on Alpha, Beta and Gamma etc factors as alpha–08, Beta–58, Gamma–36, Delta–01, Epsilon–02 where alpha is id, beta is ego, gamma represents ideal self, delta represents psychological condition and epsilon represents repressed complexes."[3]

These were taken by the Motivation Analysis Test or the School of Motivation Analysis Test (MAT, 1964 Swaney, SMAT, 1970) as human ergs or drive patterns.

> "Similarly, the behavioural performance P can be measured using the following behavioural equation.
>
> $$Pj = B_j^a A \ldots b_j^t T + \ldots b_j^d D + \ldots$$
>
> Where the b terms are behavioural indices determining the contribution of each trait to the total behaviour in question, the A's representability factors such as intelligence, verbal ability, spatial ability etc, the T's represent temperament and the Ds represent dynamic trails, covering both the ergs (E's) and the engrams (M)."[4]

According to Atkinson, the strength or motivation to perform some act is assured to be a multiplicative function of the strength of the motive the expectancy (subjective probability) that will have as a consequence the attainment of an incentive, and the value of the incentive.

$$\text{Motivation} = (\text{Motive} \times \text{Expectancy} \times \text{Incentive}).$$

We have to analyse how specific employees will react to pay incentive plans, to democratic leadership to routine jobs etc.

The job performance is influenced by ability and motivation as follows:

$$\text{Performance} = f\,(\text{Ability} \times \text{Motivation})$$

$$\text{Ability} = f\,[\text{Aptitude} \times (\text{Training} + \text{Experience})]$$

Thus, ability is largely a factor of aptitude which is related to psychological factors like motivation.

> "When an individual's productivity is lower than his ability, it amounts to corruption, as the individuals intention at that point of time is to draw more than his share of gains. Of course, when a large percentage of people do this, the total output goes down (or does not grow at the rate at which it should) as this impoverished condition leads to less and less productivity."[5]

An examination of contemporary discussions of motivation suggests that one of the major sources of misunderstanding is the failure of most writers to distinguish clearly between drives or motives, on the one hand, and habits, reactions, tendencies on the other. When psychologists first became concerned with drives, they dealt almost exclusively with the unlearned biogenic drives, and since the gap between such drives and learned reactions was large.

Concluding Remarks

Thus, motivation being a psychological and human behaviour factor differs from time to time, individual to individual, society to society and from country to country. But its broad base has been defined so that bureaucrats may not run away from accountability under the guise of fragile and vague definition of motivation. The motivation among the bureaucrats has to be created and maintained in every bureaucratic organization so that organization gives, a better output and bureaucratic psychology is kept sound and positive so that they can render required service in long tenure in the interest of the society and the State.

REFERENCES

1. Agrawal, PK, *Motivation and Indian Bureaucracy*, MD Publications, New Delhi, 1995, p 24.
2. Ibid, p 25.
3. Cattle, Raymond and B Child Dennis, *Motivation and Dynamic Structure*, John Wiley & Sons, New York (USA), 1975.
4. Ibid.
5. Chary, SN, *My India is Great*, Wheeler Publishing, Allahabad, 1997, p 90.

6

Fear Psychosis Among Bureaucrats

Attitude determines behaviour. Much of social psychology is based on this assumption. The relationship between attitude and behaviour is the foundation of representative bureaucracy. Only rarely there can be as much as 10% of the variance in that behaviour. Therefore, there is demand of representation of minorities in bureaucracy throughout the world. In USA, there is gradual increase of representation of the black, emigrant Asians in UK and other European countries, indigenous population in Africa and Latin America, the Tibetan Buddhists in China, Scheduled Caste and Scheduled Tribe population in India, Asians in the Middle-East countries and original settlers in Australia etc. The bureaucracy has become a green pasture for the educated young populace because one gets an assured salary and insurance for a reasonably good living even after retirement. Therefore, there is lot of social conflict for government jobs either overtly or covertly. None is prepared to wait for the results or output based on merit.

The protagonists of reservations in favour of minorities argue that due representation to the minorities in government jobs is itself an achievement. Let the long injustice with the minorities be first undone then only the objective analysis can follow.

Similarly, gender equality is nowadays an accepted fundamental principle of polity. There is equality between men and women. Initially, women were more represented in routine type low jobs. But now, there is increasing emphasis on women to be represented on all types of jobs. A time will come when woman-bosses will be more than the man-bosses.

Similarly, there is more representation of 'the locals' in the self-governing units of municipal areas or villages, which are in larger number. They justify saying it as bottom to top approach. However, sometimes, in the process, the national or federal interest are lost sight of and higher managerial inputs cannot flow down to the grassroots depriving them from the innovations and best practices in various fields.

A bureaucrat has to function within the conflicting claims and counter claims. A poor bureaucrat, therefore, feels being cornered or not welcome at his work place. This creates psychological barriers in his job and insecurity of his job looms large in his mind creating mental and physical disorders. If he has a superior officer who is biased against him in the societal set-up, he will not be liked by his boss. Similarly, he may be superior caste-wise or status-wise in his societal set-up, he will look down upon his boss when he will be meeting the boss. Similarly, male workers may have superiority complex vis-a-vis their female bosses. But Weber's bureaucratic organization is such that there is no place for all such feelings or emotions. If any action or behaviour not warranted by norms of the organization, it will be treated as an act of indiscipline and the bureaucrat will be accountable for his so-called unbecoming behaviour and may even cost his job.

In a bureaucratic organization, a boss is a boss howsoever rough or tough or incapable he or she may be. He is sitting on the roof top and can spit on the subordinate but if the subordinate spits, it will fall back upon him. On such well laid down principles, bureaucratic organizations operate and these keep the polities running smoothly irrespective of the political bosses who come and go. These are bureaucratic organizations which ensure proper civic supplies to the citizens including their security within the country and protection against foreign aggression. A bureaucrat doesn't and should not try to change his organization. He has to adjust or compromise his personal ideology, thinking and predicaments with the overall goal or his organizational outer circle. This of course, creates fear psychosis among bureaucrats. To cope with these adverse effects, he can resort to meditation and yoga in his personal life. A bureaucrat, after entering into bureaucracy, becomes so incompetent or useless to take up jobs elsewhere in private sector as two cultures are poles apart. This is one of the reasons why a bureaucrat becomes egoist or haughty or self-centered *inter alia* to conceal his frustration or incapacity in his working in non-government or semi-government job.

> "For the careerist public servant, of course, the ultimate sanction of political representatives i e removal from office is seldom available. But other and more subtle censors and sanctions are possible *viz* unfavourable publicity, reassignment, reduction of responsibilities, withholding of promotion, etc."[1]

In case of reservation of certain class of persons based on caste or race, it should not be excessive. The State has to bear in mind that the provision should be consistent with the maintenance of efficiency of administration.

Similarly, the persons in the same category of economic creamy layer cannot claim reservation as they are already well off in the society. If the society doesn't survive, no caste, or section can survive. Therefore, the reservation to a particular group or class has to be made considering overall interest of the society with adequate safeguards to merit and talent.

> "However, in case of reservation for women, reservation of posts up to 50% posts in favour of female candidates has been held valid in India by the Apex Court in various judgements as Article 15(3) of Constitution of India provides for special provision for women and children."[2]
>
> "Similarly, reservation of certain posts exclusively for women is valid under Article 15(3)."[3]

In the same vein, to ameliorate the condition of women in India, the Supreme Court of India laid down that sexual harassment of working women amounts to violation of the rights guaranteed by right to equality and dignity.[4] In this case the court issued detailed guidelines directions on the subject which were implemented by the government in public and private organizations with more sanctity and sincerity than the implementation of a statute.

These guidelines were issued after the incident of brutal gang rape of a social worker in Rajasthan. The Supreme Court directed that the governments and even the private sector have to work to implement the Convention on the Elimination of All Forms of Discrimination Against Women popularity known as CE DAW. It enjoins on all governments to take all appropriate measures to eliminate discrimination against women in the field of employment in order to ensure equality on basis of gender. "Equality in employment can be seriously impaired when women are subjected to gender specific violence, such as sexual harassment at the work-place. Sexual harassment includes such unwelcome sexually determined behaviour as physical contacts and advances, sexually coloured remarks, showing pornography and sexual demands, whether by words or action."[5] The court asked for effective complaints procedures and remedies, including compensation which should be provided by the employer.

The Complaints Committee should be headed by women and more than half its members should be women. Awareness of the rights of female employees in this region should be created by notifying guidelines.

The Union Government of India subsequently got passed the Sexual Harassment of Women at Workplace (Prevention, Prohibition and Redressal) Act, 2013 on the same lines which is being implemented throughout the country.

The Act enjoins upon every employer to provide a safe working environment at the work-place for women.

Coping with Innovations

There is so much innovations and diversification in the jobs performed by bureaucrats that the old guards feel sometimes lost. They require lot of training and retraining but that is also not always available at their work place.

> "The Central Government in India started the trend of setting up technology missions for organizing the execution of schemes with time-bound goals such as rural water supply and immunisation.

The mission mode entails clarity of objectives and strategies; action within a definite time-frame; an assured budget, fast track procedures, a committed team of officials, inter-sectoral effort, collective action, close monitoring; and transparent evaluation. Some States like Madhya Pradesh also set up missions, centring on areas of universal literacy, health and livelihood security in rural areas.

The second organizational solution is the creation of autonomous societies, registered under the Societies Registration Act, for the implementation of major social projects assisted by donor agencies or central ministries. Central Government had already set the trend with the agreement with States for the constitution of district rural development agencies to receive and utilise funds for specified activities, as well as district societies for various disease control programmes. The objective was to combine the flexibility and innovation of NGO with the legitimacy and authority of government support."[6]

Another innovation to tone up the sagging working of bureaucracy undertaken is application of computer technology extensively in the governance to make it faster, more objective and more transparent. E-governance harnesses information and communication technologies (ICT) such as internet, the worldwide web including social media and mobile phones to deliver public service on the mobile phone of the citizen and business, improves decision making and functioning of government and enhances efficiency of service delivery after it joins up government.

The objective of electronic governance, in government's view, goes far beyond mere computerization of stand-alone back-office operations. It is not about hardware and software but marks a fundamental change in the way government operates and interacts with citizens.

> "The Indian government has declared a 12-Point Minimum Agenda for promotion of e-governance in the functioning of ministries and departments, encompassing areas such as computer availability, Local Area Network, training and capacity building in IT, use of e-mail and e-enabling official processes such as grievance redress, setting up websites, electronic publication of information, making available forms on website, calling e-tender to weed out corruption, enabling submission of forms online, declaring results or decisions online and e-delivery of citizen services such as delivery of record-of-rights of land, electricity and water bills, transferring of wages in Banks by e-transfers in employment generating schemes, remittance of old-age and widow pensions and even students scholarships in the bank's accounts. Identification of agencies and areas of large interface with citizens and business for IT applications, such as public grievances, police and the issue of certificates and permits."[7]

The bureaucrats find it difficult to learn new innovations very fast firstly because of their lack of knowledge and secondly, because they can't come out of their firm beliefs and personal reservations, many of which are irrational. This type of conflict creates psychological problems in their personal life and is reflected in their working. As far as it can be lessened, it is better for the governmental system.

Division in Bureaucracy on the Basis of Caste

In India, Scheduled Caste and Scheduled Tribe members of bureaucracy are considered specially backward who need government patronage even after entering into the government jobs. Scheduled Caste and Scheduled Tribe (Prevention of Atrocities) Act, 1989 has come into effect to prevent atrocities or injustice to SC and ST members of the government machinery i e bureaucracy.

The Act provides that if anybody intentionally insults or intimidates with the intention to humiliate member of a SC or ST in any place within the public view or being in a position to dominate the will of a woman belonging to a Scheduled Caste or a Scheduled Tribe and uses that position to exploit her sexually to which she would not have otherwise agreed, shall be punishable with imprisonment for a term which shall not be less than six months but which may extend to one year.

The speciality of this Act is that the same punishment will be provided to a public servant who wilfully neglects his duties required to be done under the Act.

These types of statutory provisions are there in many other Acts or regulations specially providing for pecuniary fines if a public servant doesn't perform his duty within the time prescribed for his public service delivery of certain functions. For example, if a public servant doesn't issue certificate or 'no objection' on an application of a citizen in a specific transaction, within 30 days, he can be personally fined for his negligence of duty apart from departmental enquiry, proceeding or action against him. These regulations have been introduced because the citizens' grievances machinery in public offices shows a laxed response at the cost of citizen's plight in public offices. However, such statutory provisions or regulatory prescriptions will also be implemented by the superior officers in bureaucracy. Therefore, unless the bureaucratic system itself becomes proactive, nothing much can be done. But vigilant citizens and public conscious courts can certainly make a difference by pulling down few of such incorrigible officials to set examples for others. However, this is creating panic reaction among public officials but they have no other go except to obey the rules and regulations laid down by the elected governments.

The bureaucracy itself is divided sometimes on the basis of caste, community, race or colour and therefore, it is doubted whether Weber's monolithic bureaucrats can hold on to their erstwhile position of power and authority. One is dismayed when one visits a public office. The behaviour by an official is so indifferent that one feels that he is a beggar before him whereas the fact is otherwise. The public officials are paid the hard-earned money of the public and the public is their ultimate masters. The elected representatives came in between the bureaucrats and the public. They sometimes have their personal agenda apart from the mandate of the political party and the policy of the government. This creates more of tension in minds of bureaucrats. If the bureaucrat doesn't obey the orders of his political bosses, he is harassed, demoted or transferred on their behest by their crony officers who sometimes become united with them based on caste, race, place or colour.

Nuremberg Trial

After the excesses committed by the henchmen of Adolf Hitler during the Second World War, his deputies took the plea before the Tribunal that they were ordered by their superior. It is now well-settled that obeying illegal order of superior officer is not a defence. Among those condemned to death by hanging were Joachem Von Ribbentrop, his foreign minister by the International War Crimes Tribunal. It was held that subordinate is bound to obey lawful order of superior only. 'Respondent Superior' ie let the superior be responsible is not an admissible defence. Similarly, there was a Tokyo Trial for the war crimes committed mostly by the Japanese against the Chinese after the post World War II which has been published in 80 volumes, nearly 50,000 pages by the Shanghai Jiao Tong University Press that also reiterated the principle laid down in the Nuremberg Trials.

The similar situation arose in India to try the persons responsible for excesses done during emergency under the Prime Minister late Mrs Indira Gandhi by Justice Shah Commission. The Shah Commission after hearing the perpetrators of excesses during emergency mainly bureaucrats gave a report. Shah Commission suggested to take stringent actions against those bureaucrats who committed excesses beyond the call of their duties which further demoralized the already fragmented bureaucracy. It is doubtful whether due actions were at all taken against the guilty ones.

The doctrine of sovereign immunity ie King can do no wrong is not available when the State or its officers acting in the course of employment infringe a person's fundamental or basic right of life and personal liberty as guaranteed in most of the constitutions of the world.

Thus, it is like walking on sword. It is interesting to know how they perform their strenuous duties with ease and some of them even enjoy their tenure in bureaucracy and enrich themselves by making fortunes through illegal means or unwarranted practices. Latter are those public officials who not only spoil their peace of mind but also bring bad name to the bureaucracy in general. Let us divide the bureaucrats in three categories and analyse how they face fear psychosis while performing their duties.

(i) Lower Level Officials

This category will include clerks, assistants, typists and even helpers. In police forces, this category consists of constables or policeman. This is the base category on which pyramid of the bureaucratic structure is erected. If the foundation is weak, the building cannot remain in good condition for a longtime. Secondly, it will always be vibrating. Therefore, maximum attention is to be paid to this class of personnel. They require conducive working environment which will include quality of work life ie proper working place, availability of physical comfort or equipments for working, proper guidelines and effective supervision, availability of transport either by private or public for the work place and impartial boss. This class of personnel are also not highly respected in the society. They, from economic point of view, belong to lower middle class category of the society. As a result, there is always pressure on their mind to have additional income by illegal or extra means to have their better standard of living so that they can ensure better education to their children at par with the inspector's class and meet the medical needs of their families. If the government education and health facilities are easily available, after their working hours, they will concentrate in their jobs. As this class is not very highly educated, they require constant supervision and control by the class II officers. They have negative thinking about their system itself. Therefore, they are to be trained or brain-washed constantly so that they don't have fear regarding insecurity of job. Secondly, they should be made to identify themselves with higher goal of the bureaucratic organization which is the welfare of the people. They should be made to understand that if they work properly, the system itself will function smoothly and they will also be beneficiaries of its delivery of services as common citizens of the country. However, it is a difficult task and is a challenge to the managerial level of bureaucrats who are, in modern days, equipped with most sophisticated technologies of management to govern or manage properly .

(ii) Inspector Level Bureaucrats

This is the class or personnel who come in contact with the public most often. The image of the bureaucratic organization is formed by people based on their interaction with the public. They are called street level bureaucrats in USA. They are very conscious and are bridge between the base category and the higher category of officers. They are friend, philosopher and guide to the base category whereas they function as information gatherer or feedback providers to the higher category of bureaucrats. As they mingle with public, public also spoil them by offering them fast money or facilities to get their illegal work done or work done out of turn. Slowly and gradually, they become apt in the art of favouring citizens for their personal gains. They win the favour of their controlling officers by sharing a part of their illegally earned money. As a result, there is no redressal of grievances of public against the organization known as government service in public bureaucracy. The public gradually loses faith in government machinery and change the government by their voting power. As a result of change of government, the street level bureaucrats are not affected as far as they can keep their superior officers in good humour. In undeveloped and developing countries, these inspectors even develop links with the political executives bypassing their immediate controlling officers. As a result, the indiscipline becomes writ large and the public services suffer. In this way, the political executives also control the class I officers under them.

This class of personnel is not properly taken care of. They have to go for inquiry and field visits by their own transport. Their TA bills are not cleared in time. But they have to give output to their supervisory officer. Section officer or the officials incharge of an office comes within this category. Thus, the inspectors are happy people and represent happy and healthy face of bureaucracy. However, they suffer a lot when anti-corruption actions or departmental proceedings are started against them.

(iii) Class I Bureaucrats

The officers of highest class come in public focus nowadays due to proactive media who are always in search of sensational news. The bureaucrats are constantly taking decisions. Therefore, media finds ready-made material to talk about decisions by the senior bureaucrats which touch the public life directly or indirectly. The media depute investigator, to find out the process of decision-making which more or less becomes the policy announcements of the government after formal approval of the head of government elected by the people. Therefore, senior public officer, are always under lens and tense because they have stakeholders in public, party in power, minister, and their subordinates. They cannot control their subordinates like previous king or like managers in USA who have privileges because these subordinates are followers of the Minister who is immediate boss of seniormost bureaucrats and minister patronizes them to exploit them as their secret agents to know the working of the department and to increase their support base in public.

People in general are very happy when the senior bureaucrats are prosecuted for corruption. To satisfy the general sentiments of public, the senior bureaucrats are hackled and their decisions are questioned by police officials who have no insight into the intricacies of working in the government specially in economic matters. If no allegation is found against them substantially, the honest and straightforward bureaucrats are hounded by the special court for amassing wealth disproportionate to their known sources of income. This demoralizes the senior bureaucrats and the paralysis in decision-making creeps into the government. On the other hand, an innocent, innocuous or indecisive bureaucrat gets promotion and public applause.

In India it happened during the years 2012 and 2013 when the UPA-II government at the Centre was virtually paralysed. Resultantly, they lost the General Elections to Parliament in 2014. The subsequent Prime Minister Narendra Modi's first job was to awaken the bureaucracy by assuring them his full protection and ask them to take bold and impartial decisions in the interest of the country and well-being of the general public.

> "He advised the officers not to go ahead with any decision unless written orders are issued by their immediate superior."[8]

If there is no time, the Private Secretary to the Minister will confirm in writing immediately which will be subsequently confirmed by his Minister. In many cases, the ministers have gone back on their oral instructions so also there have been few instances where even senior officers have denied having instructed their subordinates to do a particular act which was not in accordance with the norms, rules, regulations or procedures. Therefore, it is very essential that there should be transparency in bureaucracy vis-a-vis public but also there should be total transparency and sincerity inside the bureaucracy itself so that *bona fide* subordinate officials are well-protected for obedience of orders of superior officers. However, it is not an easy solution. A bad superior officer may create many undefined problems, in the working like harassing him on small issues of grant of leave or advance or waive his late coming, flimsy objections that the subordinate official will find it difficult to work.

It seems that the Weber's bureaucrats are still in dilemma but at the same time, they cannot be dispensed with. Many elected bodies are under experimentation to deliver results but after some years they also fall in the same trap of bureaucratic working.

Physical Disorders Among Bureaucrats

Earlier people used to laugh away saying that mental and physical pressure on bureaucrats are parts of their job, and they have to welcome the same as hazards of the jobs. Problem with bureaucrats is that they feel that they are repository of knowledge on the subject.

Now with the expansion of IT, they have second-hand knowledge and half-backed ideas. Therefore, they fall prey to some or the other mental disorder or physical problem or disease. These may be termed as occupational diseases of bureaucrats. An occupational disease is one which is directly relatable to the performance of duties on the job. It is a subject of research. Not much work has been done in this direction. The majority of bureaucrats in earlier times used to invite these diseases themselves by resorting to unhealthy work practices and creating equal number or quantum if not more, to their opposite side of the table ie citizens or customers. But now the situation has assumed precarious proportion. The bureaucrats at all levels suffer from skin diseases, respiratory problems, insomnia, blood pressure, blood sugar, orthopaedic problems and other life-style related diseases which are directly attributable to their work. One of them is loneliness due to loss of identity and restriction on free speech and expression. The governments have to spend lot of public exchequer on keeping its machinery in order from health point of view. Therefore, efforts are to be made to reduce psychological disorders or diseases among the bureaucrats as a special drive.

Concluding Remarks

The working of bureaucrats is not so smooth as it used to be in olden days, when it was presumed that king can do no wrong. The bureaucrats had the immunity of king as they were and are the hand, mouth, ear and the eyes of the king who are now the elected representatives as a group. Even the King has no immunity. It is well-accepted that when the king is doing commercial transactions, he should be held liable as any other person doing commercial transactions. Earlier the sphere of activities of the king was limited to maintenance of law and order, administration of justice and defence of his kingdom or country. Now, the bureaucrats are asked to take the economy ahead so that the prosperity may percolate down to the last man in the society. Accordingly, bureaucrats have become multi-tasked personnel. Unlike their counterpart in private sector, they cannot move in straight line in a water-tight compartment only working for profits or gain of their employer. The employers are now millions of people who contribute to the revenue of the State and are objects of activities of the State. Thus, the bureaucrats have to perform multifarious functions in the courtyard of the society as per needs of the society which may differ from time to time and country to country. He is faced with a great challenge to change himself which is not always possible. His environment of working is also varied and may not be according to his choice.

As a result, bureaucrat suffers from many psychological and resultant physical disorders. Many of them resort to drinking and leisure loving. It is high time that the system takes care to set-up psycho therapy units for them by creating conducive work environment of working and also positive incentives and facilities like Yoga and Pranayama to improve output and quality outcome by the bureaucrats. If urgent attention is not paid to it, the bureaucracy will survive for itself and will not deliver any positive service to its intended beneficiaries ie public even at the cost of huge out go of public exchequer.

Secondly, the government is supposed to provide social and health security to its each and every citizen. The bureaucrats are also citizens. Therefore, there is nothing unusual to provide them proper health facilities over and above the general citizens so that they can discharge functions with full attention and devotion.

REFERENCES

1. Dolan, Julie and Rosenbloom, David H (eds), *Representative Bureaucracy*, ME Sharpe, New York, London, 2003, p 20.
2. Rajesh Kumar Gupta *vs* State of Uttar Pradesh, AIR 2005 SC/(2005) 5 SCC 172.

3. Union of India *vs* KP Prabhakaran (1997), 11 SCC 638.
4. Visakha *vs* State of Rajasthan, AIR 1997 SC 3011 (1997), 6 SCC 241.
5. Ibid.
6. Commonwealth Secretariat, A Profile of the Public Service of India, Commonwealth Secretariat, London (UK), 2004, p 109.
7. Ibid, p 171.
8. *Times of India*, dated 2nd November 2014.

7

Anatomy of a Bureaucrat at Work

In addition to the familiar senses, psychologists, now add two less familiar feedback or information sources ie bodily movement and outward balance or posture. There is a growing school, on reverse side, of psychological thought which believes that all physical illness is also psychological to a greater or lesser extent.

A bureaucrat is generally in permanent employment in the government. He expects some measure of independence and autonomy, a feeling of competence, achievement and self-worth, a feeling of being valued, of making contribution and of belonging because government belongs to all. When people have difficulty in coping with occupational or personal pressures, stress is generated,

> "A Civil Servant stands in the middle of the scale on occupational stress scale (Cooper, CL, 1985)."[1]

Like any other category of employee, civil servant has problems at work and domestic problems at home. If one doesn't balance the two, making of money for family in the bureaucratic job may even spoil the family members. In the process of making money, the family is not properly guided and taken care of.

Money is a top consideration for work nowadays, but in a survey in 1990 conducted in seven countries – Belgium, Britain, Israel, Japan, the Netherlands, the United States and the former West Germany (Harbez 1990),

> "The most important work goal (out of 11 possibilities) that people identified in five of these countries was 'interesting work'. In other countries, it was rated second (Netherlands) and third West Germany."[2]

Thus there is wide variety of physical as well as psychological approach to work. Let us analyse how the imaginary anatomy of a bureaucrat represents his work-situation.

The personality of a bureaucrat is like an iceberg whose ninth-tenth part is hidden within water. The bureaucrat is apt in the art of hiding his real personality. Even then, the analysts will not leave him any more as he is a very important part of the society. His decision, reaction and even mood have impact on the well-being of the society. A bureaucrat is a person who is well-grooved from his childhood to become a normal sociable adult. And then only he has qualified for the job through test examination among many other competitors which was indeed quite tough as compared to tests for many other avocation or streams. Security of job has placed government jobs on higher pedestal. He is an intelligent person who has the capacity to read the pulse of his stakeholders mainly public and to respond suitably. It is presumed that he has a large size brain which is stable and has proper input-output system inside it. In developing and less-developed countries, bureaucrats are the cream of the society. Even in developed countries, the bureaucrats are socially well-recognized. Therefore, many of the young people in spite of high salaries in private sector, prefer to join government or semi-government organizations. He however, develops negativities after joining the government because he has so many clients to oblige who have competitive demands and sometimes even rival demands. Therefore, his brain is a poor receptor of outside inputs, reflexes or light. As the whole society is his work-field, he keeps his nose sensitive to smell rumours.

But he knows his limitation as his bureaucratic organization is very powerful as compared to him. He is just like a cog in a wheel. His boss is very insensitive to his suggestions. Therefore, he wants to pose as if he has not received all the actional informations. He has big ears because he has an array of his assistants who are feeding him continuous information and giving their suggestions. But he doesn't keep his ears open to all the complaints because he knows well that he will not be able to act upon those complaints less redress them because of insensitive working of his office or organization. Therefore, he tries to stop as many complaints reaching his ears as he can. But it is not always possible. There is always a public pressure built on him to listen and to act on the complaints to the satisfaction of the complainants. This is mandate of the public who have sent their representatives over and above the bureaucrat to oversee him according to their need and aspirations. Therefore, he will not always be able to resist to obtain or to register public complaints by him. Redressal of public complaints is also one of his assigned important duties.

In such a scenario, he lives in contradictions. He desires something but does something else. He has not yet fully identified his personal goal with the mission of the organization. His personal needs or obligations are not finding full satisfaction in his job. His family obligations are not fulfilled. He has lot of peer pressure on him and pressure from his friends and relatives. As a result, a bureaucrat is not one in reality what he stands for himself. Or a bureaucrat poses himself what he is not from within. Thus he has a split personality full of contradictions. He finds difficulty in coping with occupational and personal hazards.

> "The physical consequences of not being able to resolve a stressful situation directly by using our emergency resources in-flight or fight can be very serious in fact life threatening. Increasing heart rate and blood pressure for a short term emergency only, for example, is the body's natural way of coping, but on a long term basis it is a prime cause of strokes and heart disease and can also lead to kidney damage. Increasing blood cholesterol level can lead to arteriosclerosis (hardening of arteries) and subsequent heart disease. Altering blood sugar levels over a lengthy period increasing the risk of diabetes, and slowing down the immune system leaves one vulnerable to a wide range of infections, possibly including cancer."[3]

However, some of the bureaucrats manage their stress and ride on the top of pyramid with the help of excitement and stimulation like marrying or changing the job, they use the zest to meeting new challenges. Thus, their stress becomes life enhancing and not life threatening as with mountain climbers and racing drivers, at the same time.

The bureaucrat who has supportive home environment, the effects of the stress can be greatly reduced as measured by lowered cholesterol level. Thus, his heart can be decongested. With the support of colleagues at work ie from peers, supervisors and subordinates, there will be reduction in blood pressure. The support of colleagues is more important when there is ongoing stress at work, probably because they are directly and continually involved with him. Not everyone is fortunate enough to have a warm and emotionally supporting relationships at home or at work. However, there are still ways in which stress at work can be managed or at least reduced.

> "Specific techniques can also be helpful including simple relaxation and exercise to help people feel better physically, and therefore mentally. Helping individuals deal with stress helps the organizations too. It has been calculated that every dollar spent on treating stress at work, yields an organization $ 5.52 in improved job performance (NIOSH, 1987). More complex psychological techniques can also be employed like teaching people how to be assertive to themselves without becoming aggressive, or how to plan coping strategies for future stressful situation. In addition individual clinical counselling and psychotherapy is increasingly being made available and proving helpful, for job related problems of mental health."[4] (Firth and Shapiro, 1986)

However, the Indian system of Yogasanas and Pranayama can cure the stress. Techniques and performance of Yogasanas and Pranayama are a system of self-treatment wherein the stress can be treated by the person himself as the ailment lies within him. The individual himself is responsible in both the cases, that is, for causing as well as for curing the diseases. Regular physical activities produce both psychological and physical benefits. Physical benefits are long age, less probability of heart diseases, reduced risk of protracted diabetes, less likelihood of developing high blood pressure, control of weight loss and healthy bones, muscles and joints. Secondly, a person always bubbles with confidence that he is not inferior to anybody. Finally, through arts such as music, dancing, theatre and painting, one can enhance his pleasure and nourish his psychology. Yoga is an excellent self-help tool in correcting psychological and physical disorders. The Yoga therapy is a specialized form of Yogic culture and various Yoga centres in India have developed their own systems on the basis of their experience and research. In the absence of any standardization, there is some variation in the method of therapeutic Yoga at various centres in India and elsewhere in the world. Though most of the patients are cured with only proper diet and Yoga practice, there are some cases, which are rather complicated. Some patients develop diseases and disorders on account of their false assumptions, unhealthy habits, and lack of proper knowledge about life, nature and society. In such cases, a lot of things are told to the patients, which are informative, conceptual, theoretical and also philosophical. Some of these things are spiritual whereas the other are scientific interpretation of things. This therapy suits to a bureaucrat because he has not to divulge his mental complexes to the outsider doctor. As a result, his energy level goes high with happiness and bliss generated. He finds his work interesting and conducive. He achieves required success at his work place.

When he comes out to his work-place free from stress, he deals things with iron fist and can take pleasant or unpleasant decisions commensurate with the exigencies before him consistent with his position or post in a bureaucratic organization. In a regulatory and formal organizations like the bureaucracy, firm decisions are expectedly backed by the power of sanction or reward or punishment with the decision-maker. It is a fact that bureaucrat has half-baked ideas as regards himself and even as regards the subject before him. He doesn't verify or update the advances in the society which have taken place after he has entered into the bureaucracy firstly because he is occupied with day-to-day routine unimportant jobs and secondly, because he works in a closed circuit. That may be with so many other classes of working people but a bureaucrat is more opaque to new ideas or suggestions, firstly to hide his ignorance and secondly due to his super ego. If he has requisite openness and transparency, he will be stress free himself and will be loved and respected by public at large who are his stakeholders.

Another drawback with a bureaucrat is that he has lot of space for emotion towards his family and friends inside him. He overlooks that once he has entered into bureaucracy, he has to be cent-percent objective, impartial and should conform to rules and regulations which have been laid down for many years after lot of experiences and as a result of historical evolution. Thus, he has to compromise with his personal inclinations, attachment and problems. He is being paid handsomely with an object to go out in society and solve his family problems himself with the salary he gets in the government job. This is easily said but is difficult to practise as the bureaucrat has lot of power to solve his personal problems being in the government and can take advantage of his power, position and the infrastructure at his disposal.

A bureaucrat is working in an organization which is driven by rules and regulations which are being continuously added and updated to the already voluminous kitty. Everybody is talking about the rules and regulations from morning to the evening. Intelligent and clever colleagues tilt the rules and regulations to suit the interests either of themselves or to their clients. The colleagues well-conversant with rules and regulations are regarded superior to others. Even through training and retraining, he is continuously given inputs of new executive instructions, government notifications etc which form manual or code for his working. None has time or patience to enrich his mental health or correct his psychology. He is supposed to adjust him to this continuous intake of regulations. These regulations are mostly indifferent and dry. A bureaucrat finds it difficult to apply these regulations according to people's need and with human touch.

Therefore, he faces inner conflict while working with these rules and regulations. In spite of his best and *bona fide* intentions, he will not be able to apply according to his conscious to the issue before him without risking his own career.

Secondly, regulations are so many that he may not even be aware of all of them. When he processes a note applying a particular rule, he will find that his note has been overruled by his superior applying another rule for the same set of facts and he will be brushed aside as a person lacking in proper understanding and knowledge of regulations. As a result, he will be jeered by his peers or subordinates losing his composure in his working environment. Therefore, he is non-committal to any decisions because he is not sure whether his note or approach will be approved by the top boss. A boss is always the boss. He cannot be questioned. Sometimes, his superior puts in some additional facts which were not in his knowledge. Even then, he is hauled up for his poor knowledge around though he knows well that his boss is wrong and has given the input for some ulterior purpose. He has to compromise with his boss because over-turning his notes number of times, will make his seat or himself redundant in the organization. Over and above, his decisions are subject to rule of law, statutory laws and the constitution of the country but he has not been given any code of working and conduct. He has not been imparted training in ever-growing volume of rules and regulations specially in view of increasing number of problems due to explosion of population, multiplying disputes and involvement of bureaucracy in economic matters in a big way. Everybody is seemingly in hurry in bureaucracy. The boss asks for immediate action though he may later on sleep on the file. But it is his privilege. One should appreciate the predicament of a bureaucrat in which he has to function. He dreams regulations, he reads regulations he listens to regulation, he speaks regulations and regulations only, he smells regulations, he eats regulations and vomits regulations. Thus, his life revolves around regulations only. His belly is so big that it absorbs all types of regulations flowing from different offices or quarters. In spite of having a big belly of regulations he is not certain whether he will be able to apply correct regulation to a given situation or circumstances.

In fact, in bureaucracy, the decision is multi-layer one. The file is initiated from one section with certain approach or regulation applicable. Then it is forwarded to other sections or departments which will be affected by the proposed action or circular and the opinion is sought from all those sections or departments which have expertise in that field and which will be affected by the decision under consideration. This is good because in that situation, the sections or departments which have participated in decision-making whether right or wrong, will not be able to disown that decision and will implement the decision with earnestness and sincerity. Every file invariably is sent to the finance department whether there is financial implication or not in the subject under consideration. Even the file must have noting from the finance department that there will no financial implication because there may be some hidden financial involvement in future. Sometimes, it takes so much time in decision-making that the decision itself becomes irrelevant or redundant and is given up. On the other hand, when such type of decision is notified, the section which initiated the file, is sometimes surprised itself to find that the requirement was one thing whereas the decision finally arrived at was pole apart and it was difficult to co-relate the two. Even the most powerful American President has to read his decision on dotted line though his personal opinion may differ.

Therefore, a modern bureaucrat is said to have legs made of spring so that he can tilt his collapsible legs to the desired direction as per the situation. Similarly, he has feet in opposite direction so that he can ensure physical balance as well as mental equilibrium among opposing claims or suggestions.

It is perhaps, due to foregoing working or decision-making style, a bureaucrat doesn't commit anything to his client unless the decision is finally published under the seal of the concerned government or its designated officer. Earlier it was the practice that a government order, if published cannot be changed in anyway. It was good for stability in bureaucratic functioning because elected representatives come and go but government officials are there permanently until their retirement. This power was misused by many corrupt and dishonest officials. Therefore, their decisions though already acted upon are being challenged in higher courts so as to instil fear among bureaucrat that he is not the final authority in an illegal decision whatsoever. The decision of the Indian Supreme Court in 2G Scam and Coal Scam are the reminders to the bureaucrat that he should prospectively take a decision which is legitimate within the four corners of law and as per the mandate of the constitution of the country. Earlier, these deviations were allowed only prospectively. Therefore, a bureaucrat could run away with the partial, coloured or imperfect decision after weighing pros and cons to his personal liability and gain. The Supreme Court went little out of way and found that a decision ab-initio void cannot be validated by subsequent imperfect executive notification. It has to be a proper and legal decision of the government followed by a gazette notification.

Psychological Satisfaction is More Important than Money

The idea that people at work could be treated like machines only working for wages or money, became popular with employers after Henry Ford opened his first car factory in USA in the early years of the twentieth century and is still popular in few western developed countries like USA. The early success of this method is part of industrial folklore. What is less well-known is that Ford almost went bankrupt some years later still using the same method, and indeed the Ford Motor Company has never regained its initial dominance of the market. The lesson has still not been learned by the end of the twentieth century, and it bears a lot of repeating, "you cannot just hire hands – or even brains because people always come as package deal." The human personality is quite complicated and has to be hired as a whole.

On the other hand, in the countries like Japan and South Korea, life time employment has dominance at present at least, in the car market. Its industrial set-up, apart from main furnace, assembly lines, the administration, HR and accounts departments are kin to a bureaucratic organization and their workers are more or less bureaucrats.

According to Ralph Larsen, ex-Chairman and CEO, Johnson and Johnson (1993):

> "In today's world, our challenge must be to energize and empower the talents and commitment of our people and build our success from the bottom up."

Therefore, psychological tests are not the panacea for curing deficiencies in a staff's psychology. His psychology has to be constantly nurtured through his extensive training and development techniques so that he stays happily with the organizations and organization can use his talent to the fullest extent. Psychological needs that would be satisfied are much more important to people than simply making more money. Thus, neither the psychological screening at the time of entrance nor psychological treatments which are flooded in the West, are solutions. The real solution is to make the organization pro-employee that he feels one with the organization and is immune from pressures from peers or criticism or pressure from the superior. His talent should bloom in the organization. Such an environment if created, the organization will flourish without outside efforts and maximum output will be available from every employee. Of course, it is difficult to achieve in a bureaucratic organization because the organization is antithesis of growth of employee. But the traditional values can be changed. The physical environment in government offices requires lot of improvement according to the need of the climate. Already, in bureaucracy, the monetary compensation is secondary because a bureaucrat is more or less satisfied with his social status being in government office. He has to be given assurance that his viewpoint or note in file has been duly given weightage and he has not been neglected or bypassed vis-a-vis his other colleagues in matters of promotion and postings. The merit based on objective and impartial assessment of performance, is the key for creation of the positive environment in an organization. The organization cares for him and his family by providing medical facilities or treatment to him and his family. His self-efficacy can be increased by following four strategies:

"1. Using models to teach the person to overcome difficulties.

2. Allowing the person to imagine himself or herself behaving effectively.

3. Using verbal persuasion by a trustworthy psychotherapist.

4. Teaching techniques for lowering arousal e g meditation, mindfulness, biofeedback, hypnosis, relaxation etc to increase the likelihood of more adaptive, self-efficacious thinking."[5]

In addition, pursuing one's hobby can help in enhancing self-efficacy and proper efficiency at work.

Thus, efforts done in a proper direction can mould the psychology of a bureaucrat to a positive .psychology to uncovering bureaucrat's strengths and promoting his positive functioning.

REFERENCES

1. Statt, David A, *Psychology and the World of Work*, The MacMillan Press, London, 1994, p 93.
2. Ibid, p 396.
3. Ibid, p 90.
4. Ibid, p 98.
5. Snyder, CR and Lopez, Shane J, *Positive Psychology*, Sage Publications India, New Delhi, 2007, p 178.

8

Corruption Among Bureaucrats

Corruption and bureaucrats are closely inter-linked. It is widely perceived that bureaucrats use corrupt practices especially bribery or fraud for their personal gains at the cost of State which is an offence against public at large. With regard to a bureaucrat or public servant, corruption means and includes

(i) habitual acceptance of gratification;

(ii) the receipt of any valuable thing without consideration;

(iii) misappropriation of government funds;

(iv) the abuse of position to obtain pecuniary advantage; and

(v) the possession of pecuniary resources or property in excess to one's known sources of income.[1]

Corruption is one of the most common as well as the most dangerous forms of ethical feature. It had earlier existed in one form or another in all societies at all times of history. But in recent years, it has assumed frightening proportions. It has created inefficiencies and inequities and has even created imbalance in the economy of a country infested with corruption like India, Bangladesh and Pakistan. One has to analyse their psychology why they are so corrupt.

> "Psycho analysis seeks to heal. Therapy is to repair damage that disables full functioning today due to an injury of childhood. Full functioning is modelled as the integrated meshing of ego, super ego and id: mastery, conscience and energy."[2]

However, super ego can regulate ego and id following the communal norms. Therefore, in case of bureaucrats, their super ego has to be focused.

Causes of Corruption

Bureaucrats indulge into corruption due to one of the following reasons or for more than one reason;

(i) The pay scales of civil servants are poor so much so they cannot afford to run their families. To tide over genuine financial problems, they resort to bribe taking.

(ii) Bureaucrats are offered speed money to expedite their decision or to push up the file to avoid delays. No harm is caused to government's interest.

(iii) Bureaucrats who are basically honest, are tempted by the private officials to accept cordial gifts initially. The practice of accepting gifts is ultimately converted into accepting bribe as the bureaucrat and his family, for having a better style in life, is caught into that trap unaware of its evil consequences in future. However, small gifts or tips as tokens of appreciation without expectation of benefits in return, cannot be termed as corrupt practices.

(iv) Bribe is given to exercise discretion by a bureaucrat in favour of a private person as per law or rules. This refers to wide spread corruption in various quasi-judicial authorities and government agencies where the bureaucrats have discretion without rules or guidelines being prescribed to exercise their discretion.

(v) There are bureaucrats who enters into government jobs after paying bribe. There are others who from the beginning decide to go for corruption as it will give them status in the society. Corruption is rooted in acquisitive or artificial society where status of individuals and position of their families is judged by what they possess rather than by what they are. The acquisition of wealth has become *sine qua non* of life. People indulge in acquiring wealth without caring for the means they adopt.

(vi) There are bureaucrats who have no principles or values in life. They indulge into corruption to satisfy their lust for money without knowing that money is a means and not an end in itself. They connive with everybody including politicians to make money and even become their conduits or collaborators to make money by hooks or crooks. These people have stopped listening to their soul and flagrantly indulge into corrupt practices until they are caught by anti-corruption agencies and are prosecuted and jailed.

Their psychology becomes quite negative to the jobs they are doing. They consider their jobs as instrument to earn money rather than means for public service or public welfare.

(vii) There are bureaucrats who have come to government job due to reservation or otherwise. They compare with their counterpart in society and in bureaucracy and will compete with them as regards their status in the society and make good by earning money in their jobs.

(viii) There are inadequate laws and anti-corruption or vigilance bodies to catch such bureaucrats. On the other hand, top level bureaucrats and top politicians present bad examples of high level corruption. Thus, the bureaucrats find it easy to indulge into corruption.

(ix) Few bureaucrats find that indulging into corruption is a beneficial adventure from cost-benefit analysis. People get rid off charges of corruption by spending the ill-earned money on hiring reputed lawyers. Thus, they save surplus money to have stylist and good life even after retirement in addition to pension available in government jobs.

(x) There is lot of security provided in government job. Therefore, over assurance to bureaucrats impel them to go for such adventure of corruption.

(xi) Honest officers are not respected in bureaucracy nor in society. There is therefore, no incentive to maintain high standards of honesty and integrity and transparency by the self-conscious bureaucrats.

Tackling Corruption

Corruption among bureaucrats cannot be tackled without co-operation from the bureaucrats. There is a majority of bureaucrats who are in favour of weeding out corruption but they are shy to come forward in support of the campaign as power of corrupt bureaucrats is writ large. The causes of corruption have to be remedied through sustained efforts in bureaucracy or Civil Service.

In USA, the pay of bureaucrats nowadays is at parity with private sector earnings. As a result, bureaucrats who wield so much power do not feel inferior to their counterparts in private sector in a society in which pay is one of the indicators of status symbol.

The civil servants are asked to take decisions in matters where there is conflict of interests. Most developed countries forbid civil servants from involvement in decisions in which they have a financial interest. In most of the cases, both bureaucrats and top political appointees must disclose their financial assets to a public agency earmarked by the government. In post-colonial Africa, many countries encouraged public officials to engage in business activities that overlapped with their official duties. They try to take up second job outside government jobs and try to fill the gap by accepting illegal pay offs. For example, in Zaire in 1986, salaries made up only 33% of the income of officials. In Tanzania wages and benefits averaged 40% of household expenses and the government encouraged officials to seek outside employment.

> "After many years have passed, the Civil Service will be disproportionately stuffed with two bands of workers ie low

> productivity workers who are not employable in seemingly comparable jobs in the private sector and those willing to accept bribes."[3]

Even generous perks would not close the pay gap in all countries including in Latin American countries. Conflict of interest and corruption seriously undermine State efficiency. Widespread conflicts exist in Russia, Eastern Europe and China.

To speed up a genuine disposal of file like routine job to pay taxes or fees, the public doesn't see the corruption as endangering the system as the customer or public itself is interested to take advantage out of turn. So also the efforts by the private citizens to tempt government officials to accept bribe should be equally punished which has not been done in many countries. India has happily done by bringing change in law.

The rules in USA regarding anti-corruption are very tough as these contain civil and criminal sanctions whereas French and Canadian solutions focus more on administrative than criminal remedies.

In Italy, strong anti-corruption measures are in practice. As a consequence, the bureaucrats have slowed down decision-making. This is more harmful for the polity. The government business and economy should move fast. If it is required, the commission should include indecision or delay in decision-making which amounts to corruption. In law, commission and omission are the two sides of the same coin.

Bureaucrats are taken on roll of government with lot of discretionary power. No regulation can do away with their discretion. The only way out is to train, retrain them in values or ethics in administration so that they exercise their discretion in a just and equitable manner. Avoidance of law should be made punishable if it is converted into a crime under the criminal law of the country. The delay in decision-making should be equally punishable. If it is made so, the bureaucrats and their collaborators will not be able to plan for the corrupt deal which always requires lot of planning and thinking.

Controlling Bureaucratic and Political Corruption

In cases of incurable and determined corrupt officials and political executives, independent judicial and prosecutional institutions are only safety valves.

> "An honest and well-respected judiciary has a special role to play in resisting corrupt governments and maintaining the rule of law. In Italy, for example, independent magistrates were central to the persistence of the recent anti-corruption investigations and prosecutions. In India, the Supreme Court pushed forward a corruption investigation that the government wanted to quash. The Court removed the Prime Minister from control of the federal agency (CBI) investigating the issue. In Spain the Supreme Court forced officials to reveal the way secret Interior Ministry accounts were used. It held that public officials could not use State security as a defence if criminal activities are suspected. In Korea, an appellate court upheld the conviction of two former Presidents on corruption charges (Kim and Kim, 1977). In Brazil, the Supreme Court insisted that the congressional impeachment of President Collor be held in public and that each congressman's vote be fully open. These demands helped keep the process honest and led to the dismissal from office of a blatantly corrupt President. (Geddes and Ribeiro Neto, 1992)"[4]

If such high officials are punished for indulging into corruption, naturally psychology of bureaucrat in general will have ingrained fear to tread on the path of corruption that corruption does not ultimately pay. This will resound in the mind of bureaucrats and they will make up the mind or psychology not to indulge into corruption. If powerful bureaucrats or politicians could not defend themselves how could the ordinary bureaucrat withstand against the State power of prosecution and punishment which he had witnessed during his long career in bureaucracy and had seen many of his so-called powerful colleagues breaking down ultimately and becoming mental patients. Their ill-gotten money is spent on defending court cases involving graft cases against them and to have their treatment with specialized doctors.

United Nations Convention Against Corruption

UN Convention, 2005 prescribes a series of measures for preventing corruption, which include formulating and implementing effective anti-corruption policies and practices, constituting preventive anti-corruption bodies; adopting transparent system for recruitment, promotion etc of civil servants, establishing criteria of candidature for election to public office and ensuing transparency in the funding of candidature for elected public office/political parties; establishing code of conduct for public officials, establishing systems based on transparency, competitive and objective criteria in public procurement and management of public finances, public access to information, preventing opportunities of corruption among members of judiciary, enhancing transparency and proper conduct of business in the private sector, active participation of community-based organizations in fighting against corruption and instituting regulatory and supervisory regime for financial institution in order to deter and detect money laundering.

Surprising UNO has reached to the conclusion that even their loans to the developing countries cause more burden on those economies because the aid money is misappropriated by the unscrupulous contractors in connivance with bureaucrats at all levels. As a result, UN agencies have withdrawn many aided projects all over the world.

In such a global scenario, bureaucrats have to decide all over the world whether they want to lead their professional life as per code of conduct or to disturb their mental peace and equilibrium by indulging into corrupt practices and to expose themselves and their ill-gotten assets to public gaze, criminal prosecution and seizure by the same government of which they have been part and parcel. If the bureaucrats escape from the departmental action by their erstwhile brethren in bureaucracy, and dilatory judiciary, the media and public opinion will drag them into dragnet of exposure. Their patrons ie the top bureaucrats and top political executives have become so unpopular with public, because of their corrupt practices and inability to control corruption of their subordinates, that they will not be able to provide them protection umbrella or shelter. This is the greatest contribution of today's Information Technology exposure specially proactive social media like Facebook etc that public in general have the last judgment to pass on any event of public interest and the persons-in-authority cannot overlook their exposure and comments. If the media and public opinion are not attended to, some NGOs will go to the courts and file criminal case or Public Interest Litigation against corruption. As per principle of jurisprudence, any member of public can file criminal case specially in matters where public interest is involved. As bureaucrat is a public servant, his each and every action is related to public interest as he draws his pay, salary or compensation from the State exchequer which is made of the contributions from public at large. Therefore, every bureaucrat is also directly accountable to every member of public. A corrupt official will not be able to manage his misdeeds as there is an unending chain to be satisfied which will not be cost-effective for him. Misdeeds of corruption also come clearly in public domain through exercise of right to information.

Even undemocratic rulers are likely to be sensitive to public opinion if they wish to avoid civil unrest. A free press is a good check, especially in undemocratic countries that lack other means of constraining politicians and bureaucrats. Ultimately media will fail because media will focus on lucid scandals to increase their ratings and may not have any real interest in reforms that would reduce the flow of corruption stories for them to cover.

In that case, conscious individuals and groups will push for change. Thus, there seems to be no escape for corrupt bureaucrats from the dragnet of law and public censure. In this way, the psychology of bureaucrats will not support for corruption. It is a different matter that a bureaucrat indulges into corruption suppressing his inner voice or psychology. In that case, he will have to stand on trial as an ordinary criminal. As far as society is concerned, the bribe money or black money is mostly utilized in ostentatious expenditure and in unproductive purposes. It is even sometimes, used to finance illegal crimes of terrorism, drug and human trafficking and even for changing democratically-elected governments.

The Indian Scenario

After the independence, the corruption slowly grew in India. Initially, Members of Parliament and Members of Legislative Assemblies (MLAs) of States were not public servants as per the Indian Penal Code. But later on, they came within the definition. It also covered Panchayat representatives and municipal bodies chiefs. Thus, the Indian Penal Code and the Prevention of Corruption Act, 1988 covers all important public officials. Now, even the Prime Minister of India after retirement can be questioned for his actions which came under the definition of corrupt practices. But the practice of corruption also prospered and now it covers all walks of life in India. Even the ex-Prime Minister Rajiv Gandhi was named in purchase of Bofors guns from Switzerland. Ex-Chief Minister of Bihar Lalu Prasad Yadav, ex-Chief Ministers of Karnataka and Tamil Nadu were behind bars for some misappropriation of government funds or the other. In matters of misuse of funds during organizing Commonwealth Games in New Delhi in 2010, its Chairman Suresh Kalmadi was behind bars. In 2G Spectrum scandal, the then Telecom Minister Raja from DMK was jailed along with his Secretary Siddhartha Behuria. Its earlier Secretary Shyamal Ghosh was also jailed for allegedly conniving with his ex-Minister Pramod Mahajan. In Coal Scam, even the ex-Coal Minister and the then Prime Minister along with honest Coal Secretaries HC Gupta and PC Parekh are being summoned by the Special Court even after their retirement. In a similar vein, few of the close aide ministers like Babu Singh Kushwaha of ex-Chief Minister of Uttar Pradesh Ms Mayawati are resting in jail for assisting in bribery.

> "Bureaucratic corruption pervades the Indian administrative system with widespread practice of bribery, nepotism, and misuse of official position, and resources."[5]

In spite of cognizance of major corruptions, scandals or fraud, by the Supreme Court of India, the corruption at the top as well as at the grass-root level has not abated considerably. Every politician who wins an election in India seeks for money through whatever way as he is elected after spending lot of money in election and even by bribing the voters. As a result, when he gets some position in government, he tries to compensate himself suitably and tries to collect fund for the next election and even for his generations to come. If any honest or straightforward officer comes in his way, he is hell bent on him. As a result, there is demotivation among bureaucrats. Even senior bureaucrats with emotion have committed suicides like Shri HR Singh, Principal Secretary, in UP Government and recently a young IAS officer in Karnataka. Sometimes, senior officers are sandwiched between the minister and his collaborators at the lower levels. As a result, an officer loses interest in his job. He is also transferred now and then causing lot of dislocation to himself and his family.

In States like UP, transfers have become a big industry for ministers who are not very enlightened and have no commitment to the mandate of the party in power. They are very particular about personal gains and have an army of his followers and even musclemen to pressurize the bureaucrats to toe their line and facilitate their channel of illegal gratification.

Bureaucrats are harassed in their day-to-day work in granting them leave, allowances and even their appraisals are adversely affected. As a result, a bureaucrat loses all chances of future promotions. He is transferred to non-important assignments or to a godforsaken place which puts him in ridicule before his colleagues or acquaintances. Consequently, a bureaucrat is dejected from the system and his psyche or personality is shattered beyond redemption. People say that in such a scenario, only the corrupt bureaucrat enjoys the fruits of governance in league with the political executive. However, he is also brought to book when the political executive is defeated in election or is out of power or secondly when the political executive or his patron refuses to acknowledge or disowns that he had instructed the bureaucrat to do the job.

Thus, a bureaucrat in the present day scenario in India, specially in States like UP, is bewildered and is disarrayed as to which way he should go. Present regime under the Prime Minister Narendra Modi is trying to infuse confidence in him so that the economy moves on and there are no stumbling blocks due to paralysis in policy-making and decision-taking. In any case, bureaucrats are duty bound to take decisions whatsoever way they like. They cannot put country to ransom. It is upon them to adjust their psychology or inner strength to keep the system going on. Administration or bureaucracy is their system and they are responsible and accountable for its proper functioning.

REFERENCES

1. Government of India, Legislative Deptt, Ministry of Law and Justice – The Prevention of Corruption Act, Section 5.

2. Ralph P, Hummel, *The Bureaucratic Experience: Post-Modern Challenge*, KW Publishers, New Delhi, 2008, pp 109-10.
3. Rose-Ackerman, Susan, *Corruption and Government: Causes, Consequences and Reforms*, Cambridge University Press, Cambridge (UK), 1999, p 73.
4. Ibid, pp 151-52.
5. Bansal, Dr Virendra, *Corruption in Indian Politics and Bureaucracy*, Swastik Publications, Delhi, 2012, p 84.

9

Ethics of Bureaucrats

Psychology is the mental factors whereas sociology is the study of the development, structure and functioning of the human society. Ethics is moral philosophy. The ethics of bureaucrats seeks to combine both so that overall good of the people can be achieved which is also the goal of each society or nation.

Many thinkers like Karl Marx of the world believe that bureaucracy can do no good to the society and it will wither away in due course of time. But the bureaucracy has not withered away from any political system prevalent in the world. In fact, every time it is criticized, it becomes more powerful and flabby.

People nowadays are more interested in quick gains and delivery of services unmindful of the debate whether bureaucracy will survive or not. It is an accepted fact that bureaucracy is the system which is capable of delivering quick results to the public. Therefore, we shall now analyse how this machine or instrument can be more active and fast responsive.

Ethics in bureaucracy can make this all powerful organization closer and friendlier to people. Ethics means code of conduct. The code of conduct is well-defined for every public servant or a bureaucrat before he enters into the government job. In fact, he is made to swear to abide by the code of conduct which if followed in major part, can do wonders.

The scriptures of all world religions contain pearls of wisdom how one should behave in governance of people. *Gita* says that doing one's duties efficiently is Yoga. 'Yoga Karmasu Kaushalam' which is the motto of many public services in India. *Gita* further says:

> "One ought to understand what is duty and what is forbidden in the regulations laid down by the scriptures. Knowing such rules and regulations, one should behave accordingly."
>
> (*Bhagwad Gita*, Chapter XVI, Verse 24)

For bureaucrats, scriptures are their code of conduct or regulations. This understanding leads to the righteous path. The righteous path in Hindu religion is called Dharma and it is Dharma which sustains this world and all organizations on earth. Dharma is the path of least resistance. Yoga leads one to a happy and blissful life. Any other path adopted, will encroach upon the other person's Dharma or way and it will generate conflict and violence.

Ethics of bureaucrats will encompass following constituents.

Constituents of Ethics

(i) Obligation to the Constitution

The public servant vows to conform his actions to the Constitution of the country which is the basic source of all rules and regulations of bureaucracy. Accordingly, every bureaucrat has to uphold the Rule of Law and respect for human rights which are enshrined in the Constitution. He is supposed to be objective and impartial. He should implement the policies, decisions and actions taken in the public interest by a duly constituted government. He comes in conflict with his working when firstly he has his own personal agenda away from the government; secondly, when he is asked to do something illegal or against the prescribed rules and regulations. In the former case he should be prepared to pay the price for his wrong mental frame. In the latter case, there is a grievance redressal system and he can approach his superior officer and will not be personally liable for such an action by recording his objections/reservations as per rules in vogue.

(ii) Restriction on Right to Free Speech and Expression

Public servants have restrictions to comment upon government policies and working to maintain political neutrality of public service.

(iii) Conflict of Interest

Public servants are supposed to disclose their personal interest or intimacy if it is calculated to benefit any particular person or party. Thus, a bureaucrat has to be very cautious in his conduct which adversely affects his psychology and restricts growth of his personality as a social person.

(iv) Responsiveness to the Public

Bureaucrats have to be responsive to public as they are the meeting points between the government and public. They have pious duty to meet public grievances. The public forms opinion about the functioning of government from the interaction with them. The right has been ensued to the public through enactment of Right to Information Act in many countries like India.

(v) Accountability

The bureaucrats are accountable to the superior officers and the Ministers in terms of output and quality of service, timeliness, courtesy and observance of rules and procedure. Departmental action can be taken against them for violation of their duties including reduction in their rank, cut in salary, suspension and even dismissal from the service. Apart from civil action or departmental action, officers have been and can be hauled up and punished for their intentional connivance in illegal activities including corruption and they can be prosecuted and can be jailed. Their properties gained from corruption can be seized and put to public use so that corruption doesn't become a profit venture. In some countries like China and dictatorship-ruled country like North Korea, bureaucrats can be hanged if they are found to have indulged in serious corruption cases. Thus, bureaucrats have to be very cautious in their functioning. This makes their psychology full of fear and insecure. In such an environment, a person cannot have full bloom of his personality and cannot give his best to the organization. But it is bad for good persons but is required for the dishonest and the manipulative who are potential threat to the well-being of organizations, they are working in.

(vi) Non-Abuse of Official Position

The bureaucrats are required to observe, avoid wastage and extravagance as they are the trustees of society. They should not abuse official position to obtain a benefit for themselves or for someone else, in financial or other forms. Thus, a bureaucrat is like Ceaser's wife who has to be above suspicion which is easy to say but very difficult to observe.

(vii) Ethical Values at the Top Level

The higher or top level in bureaucracy has to be more careful while observing code of conduct. Their conduct or perceived conduct not only effects the bureaucratic organization but also the public at large who are always watching them. The moral leadership has to come from people at the top. Many ideologues prescribe higher punishment for them as one goes higher in the ladder, his probity influences larger segment. Their decisions have larger recurring results and percolate down to the lowest levels. Therefore, they should not connive with the political executives for the disadvantage of the public or organization or government. The political executives as public servants should be equally punishable if not more. They should not be allowed to take shelter under the parliamentary or legislative privileges or prerogatives.

Bureaucratic Ethics in Practice

A bureaucrat who enters into the public service has high ideals and lot of expectations. He has positive psychology when he enters into the government job. He has first mental shock when he finds that situation on the ground is altogether different. His boss asks him to do certain things which he is not bound by rules to carry out. From the day one, he finds it difficult to tackle his boss in a free and fair manner. The boss or his superiors create lot of tension in his mind or psychology which he has to face or fight out alone. As a result, either he surrenders to the wishes of his superior officers or decides to fight against him to keep his morale high. In any case he compromises with his psychology and becomes a *status quo* man.

At the second stage of his working, his practical psychology adapts to the practical situations beyond control of a single bureaucrat. He develops a negative psychology gradually and becomes indifferent to the work or job. He doesn't rationally analyse that the boss or the superior can contribute only about 17% of his total tension. He is still free to work in 83% of his field of work with freedom and initiative. In fact, the public comes in contact with 80% of routine work by bureaucrats where there is no interference either by the superior or by the political superior. He only has to be blamed because he makes a hill out of a mole of problems.

The third stage of a bureaucrat's psychology is very dangerous whereas either due to frustration or due to his sweet will, he loses all touch with the norms and ethical standards of his service and indulges into rampant illegal activities either all alone or in connivance with his peer, superior officer or the political higher ups. In this situation, his psychology is destructive either to satisfy his ego for money or power to project himself high before the family or in the society which he actually is not. This unhealthy competition in a bureaucratic organization gives rise to chain reactions.

> "Low ethics, today, is no doubt a world wide phenomenon but its effects are most precarious in developing countries, like India, as these are vulnerable economics. The country's policy-makers must realize that its economic and social costs are virtually

> devastating; it demoralizes the Civil Service and adversely affects its performance. It must be fought. Otherwise, the society will be forced to resort to extraordinary measures, like violence, to deal with the evil."[1]

No country is immune from the moral disarray which we have seen recently. Even in the People's Republic of China, which was hailed as a paragon of public virtue and morality because very few cases of public service's unethical activities and corruption have been reported. One of the reasons is that the punishment for such acts of bureaucrats in a communist country is very severe and quick. Even bureaucrats and political executives and Minister are hanged or given life imprisonment. Therefore, the fear is instilled in the minds of bureaucrats so that they abhor such practices.

Sir Ivor Jennings has observed:

> "The most elementary qualification demanded of a minister is honesty and incorruptibility. It is, in addition, necessary not only that he should possess this qualification but also that he should appear to possess it."[2]

Most of the countries have public service code or law to regulate the conduct of bureaucrats.

> "The UK Civil Service code recognizes that Civil Services are accountable to the public and need to meet the highest possible standards in all that they do. Their core values are: integrity, honesty, objectivity and impartiality."[3]

USA has the Ethics in Government Act, 1978. Accordingly, members of the upper levels of the executive branch (including the President, Vice-President, and other high ranking officials) must file annual financial disclosure reports. In Australia, the

Public Service Act, 1999 mandates that bureaucrats should avoid any conflict of interest among others. Canada has Values and Ethics Code 2003, for the Public Service to enhance public confidence in the Civil Service. In Singapore, the Prevention of Corruption Act has done wonders to make small country of Singapore as corruption free. The European Ombudsman has issued the European Code of Good Administrative Behaviour. Even the United Nations has issued an International Code of Conduct for Public Officials in 1996.

If this is done then large number of dictators or military rulers will not dictate or force the bureaucrats or their subordinate police or army officers to executive their illegal or unethical orders. It will save the psychology of bureaucrats being converted into base psychology. In many countries, a widespread sense of moral disarray exists, neither industrial nor Third World countries are exempt from this disarray. Everywhere instances are on the rise detailing the collapse of standard and quality of service. This has contributed to the public cynicism; but at the same time, public is clamouring for a new set of bases for public morality and decent moral standards.

In a similar vein, the Supreme Court of India in Veerappan case against Karnataka Government held that if government cannot tackle such criminal menace, they must leave.[4]

> "Generally speaking in practically all critically surveys, opinions, etc of the Civil Service (IAS), some common trends can be discerned. It is commonly believed that civil servants have no vision beyond self-advancement. They have no self-generating strategy of change of oneself and for shaping the environment. The file is a personal zamindari (feudal lordship). And finally, they are presently starting a total intellectual, emotional and spiritual

> stagnation. The value base of the service has consequently became gentle low."[5]
>
> "The tasks of administrators in the new millennium are likely to be increasingly tasks of refinement; considering all the relevant factors, ignoring irrelevant factors, and in many cases, making decisions that set complexities of infinite sheds of grey into frameworks that are increasingly expected to be black and white. Nolan's Committee's Seven Principles of Public Life are: selflessness, integrity, objectivity, accountability, openness, honesty and leadership."[6]

However, everything is not lost. The bureaucrats in spite of all limitations have demonstrated tremendous agility around the world in cases of emergency situations like earthquakes, sunamis, floods, droughts, wild fire, severe accidents and war or war like situation against terrorism. This agility and sincerity and seriousness has to inform in normal working of the bureaucrats to keep public anger against them at bay. Public has inseparable relationship with bureaucrats. Therefore, the only solution is to improve upon the working standards of bureaucrats by adhering to proper ethical norms and professional standards at all times in all circumstances whatsoever. They should be ethical, caring and transparent. It will regenerate people's faith in them and they in turn, will flourish in their personal life by maintaining proper mental make-up and by enjoying internal happiness.

REFERENCES

1. Maheshwari, SR, "Ethics for Civil Service in India" in *IJPA*, July-Sept 1995, p 461 and in *Good Governance*, SL Goel, Deep & Deep Publications, New Delhi, 2007, pp 253-54.

2. Khanna, HR, "Ethics in Public Life: Issues and Remedy" in *IJPA*, July-Sept 1995, p 357 and in *Good Governance*, ibid, p 268.
3. Mathur, BP, *Ethics for Governance*, Routeledge, New Delhi, 2014, pp 287-88.
4. Dwivedi, OP, "Administrative Theology" in *IJPA*, July-Sept 1990, pp 418-19, ibid, p 25.
5. Brig Sen, Shekhar and Bhattacharya Pradip, "Ethics in Administration" in *I am Sorry: Indian Bureaucracy Cross Roads*, Dr PK Agrawal and N Vittal (eds), Manas Publications, New Delhi, 2008, p 59
6. Chapman A Richard (ed), *Ethics in Public Service for the New Millennium*, Ashgate Publishing, England, 2000, pp 230-33.

10

Psychology of Bureaucrats: The Inner Voice

The bureaucrat is said to be the egoist person. But ego is the root of one's psychology. It creates an image of itself which puts one different from others. The ego defines one's personality and is a highly dynamic concept. It depends on factors on one's environment, experience and will-power when one joins the government, he brings with him experiences of his past. If a person comes from the lower middle class, he will be down to earth. A bureaucrat from the middle class knows the roots but tries to be in the upper class. The bureaucrats who come from economically middle class, constitute the bulk of bureaucracy or officialdom. They are the most vocal and represent the bureaucracy. The bureaucrat from the upper class maintain their class identity and are self-oriented and career-minded from the beginning. They don't have much commitment to the job or to the mission of the organization. The economic characteristics of the Indian bureaucracy is of the Indian middle class. The pay, perks or status, one gets in bureaucracy except the fourth class or 'D' group employees, make one to belong to the middle class.

The lower class or lower middle class and upper class bureaucrats have their rigid ideologies and thinking. They believe in free life and do not bind themselves with values. They compromise whenever opportunity is offered to them. It is middle class whose psychology can be moulded according to the environment and their experiences. If the bureaucrat gets a good environment, he tries to put his best. He has an urge to learn. He is one who fights for the cause of the downtrodden in the society and is basically patriotic and loyal. But he will like to keep his job security at all costs because he has nothing to fall back upon. If he has sad experience during his early formation period of service by facing threats to his job, he will compromise with his principles in life. Service is the beautiful wife with him. Any ill eye to his dear wife can shake him totally. In any case either he will come out of his fiery test or will succumb to pressure or adverse situation. At the same time, he often compromises with his wife at home for her demands of luxury goods and stylish life. Thus he is under tremendous pressure at home and at the work place.

As a result, his emotional balance breaks down and he becomes subject to diseases and becomes burden to the society. His will-power is also formulated on the basis of his experience in the existing environment of the bureaucratic organization. However there are a few exceptions in every class who have their already well-firmed up will-power or mission which is not deviated under any adverse situation.

These people are winner in the set-up. They develop the psychological identity of being a winner. They manage their emotions and state of minds in areas where most people fail. For example in the powerful bureaucratic set-up, one cannot have frontal fight. One has to wait for chance and opportunity and then to strike with all powerful strokes. One has to go slowly up the ladders, sometimes compromising with the small things with a view to do big things later on. In case of interference or action by bureaucratic or political bosses, one has to accept with a pinch of salt as part of professional hazards and then accumulate adequate capability to strike back positively. Negative thoughts or actions generate frustration and depression everywhere whereas positivism creates a happy and workable environment. The winner is a 'yes man' to opportunities not the 'yes man' to the wrong doing even of the bosses.

One has to manage his ego. An inflated ego often comes into conflict with other persons because in order to justify the volume of his ego, he has to claim credit for achievement which may be result of hard work done by other people and not by himself. At the same time, he has to deny responsibilities for a failed action. The right size ego can be achieved by adopting right attitude in life.

The middle class bureaucrat has lot of competition. In the same office environment, one works successfully whereas the other fails. Even two twins are not the same in performance.

One has not to depend much on legacies, past happenings, actions performed and the results thereof. One has to constantly strive to work hard without expectation of results. Work is its own reward and brings satisfaction and due results creating enviable environment in life.

It is this class, which can change the colour of the bureaucratic organization. To tap them properly, the organization should have objective appraisal system, well laid down and declared transfer policy, HR system, motivational climate and availability of basic physical facilities at the work-place. If this is done, not only the bureaucratic organization will achieve its mission, the bureaucrat will also carry good psychology at home which will have positive impact on his family of four or five persons helping to create a better society to live in.

11

Do Private Sector Employees Have a Different Psychology?

– Parvez Dewan

Case 1: ITDC

It was my first day in the government-owned India Tourism Development Corporation. Two senior managers from the publicity division came up to me, their faces downcast. They had been 'chargesheeted' for letting some magazine use a photograph of an Indian tourist attraction from the ITDC photo-library without their senior's permission.

I was stunned by this pettiness. What were we keeping photographs in our photo-bank for? To lay eggs? To gather dust? Any publication that publishes an ITDC-approved picture of an Indian tourist attraction is promoting it. Isn't that why the ITDC was maintaining a photo-bank? If due permission had not been obtained that was a minor matter. At most those managers could have been gently advised, verbally, to seek permission in the future.

But the ITDC had (and continues to have) a culture of 'chargesheeting' competent officers (and, sometimes, changing official 'notings' to favour those who might be guilty). No wonder it performs so much worse than its potential.[1]

With attitudes like these, aren't Indian bureaucrats sick?

Yes, many, far too many, are. But not because they are bureaucrats. They are like this because they are Indians – Indians of a certain type. And that type is not limited to the government bureaucracy.

There is this highly successful Indian private sector hotel chain. It is NOT run by some 'lala', but entirely by career hoteliers and managers. They have a first rate golf course in Gurgaon. A few years after the ITDC incident I was working on the Incredible India calendar and decided to give each of India's 36 States a page that showed some tourist attraction that would impress international readers. Haryana's greenest and most picturesque attractions were its 'signature' golf courses.

However, my ministry received a stern email from the Vice-President in charge of that golf course asking us not to use a picture of the course. In effect, he did not want his company's golf course to get free publicity (and *de facto* government recognition) through the only Indian calendar distributed, and by the thousand at that, throughout the world.[2]

What is the difference in the psychology of the naysayers of the government-owned ITDC and this private company?

None.

And what do they have in common?

Both are Indians with a certain psychology.

Case 2: Telephone Companies

At least once on every single day, while I was working on the Internet, a service for which I paid the government-owned MTNL, my concentration would be disturbed by a badly-designed box slowly creeping up the screen of my computer, trying to get me to buy some product of theirs that I did not want. I did not have the option of pressing the 'x' button to close the box till it had crawled to the top of the screen, and it took forever to do so. Till then I had to stop all my other work and gaze at this unwanted promotion, which was, ironically, being offered in the name of 'good governance'.

Isn't the MTNL evil?

Yes, it is. But compared to the private sector Aircel it is almost nobility itself.

Aircel shatters your concentration not through some creepy-crawly slithering silently, but through the loud, tinny ring of a 1950s style telephone, which does not stop ringing till you come rushing from whichever part of the house you are in to shut the sound. My records show that this has been happening, on average, once in two days.

When we are paying for a service why should we have to suffer their intrusive ads?

Take legal VHS, CDs and DVDs of Hollywood films. The whole screen has only the image that the film's makers intended. Then why should we Indians have to tolerate the DVD manufacturer's logo on the top right hand corner of the image? I brought this to the notice of the owner of the company that, in 1987, had the biggest presence in the legal videos of Hindi-Urdu films. His ancestors and he have been major industrialists for generations. They move in the smartest circles of Mumbai. They are proud of their US and other western education. Then why can't they take note of international practices and follow them?

Because they (and the CD/DVD companies that came after them) are Indians with a certain psychology. Why, then, should we single out government bureaucrats?

Case 3: Bureaucratic Objections and Queries

Bureaucrats are, rightly, castigated for the most exasperating objections and, often, senseless queries that they subject the public to before giving them their right.

I wanted to shift my Airtel (this time it is Airtel with a 't') cellphone connection from Delhi to Jammu, as soon as this facility was announced by the government. First, Airtel's website took a few weeks to inform users how to 'port' their phone number. Finally, I was able to apply when they did. Immediately I started receiving calls from Airtel asking me why I wanted to 'port' my number. Each time I would explain, the first few times with patience and then with irritation, that I had nothing against Airtel but I had shifted my residence. The queries did not stop. Each time it was the same question. Obviously, the private sector Airtel's left hand did not know what its right hand had already done.

The number did not get 'ported' despite my sending a request by SMS to the number they had given. On repeated inquiry they informed me that several documents (proof of residence, passport photocopy etc) were needed. Fair, but then why blame the bureaucracy for asking for too much documentation?

I had been with Airtel for eleven years and had this particular number for nine years. My department kept changing during all these years and each would pay my bills. During some spells, including the nine months immediately preceding the port request, I had paid the bills myself. Even if they did not have the old records at least the immediately preceding months' records should have been seen by them. But they arbitrarily decided that my phone belonged to one particular department (not the one during whose tenure the number had been issued, which would have at least made sense) and wanted a 'no objection' from this department, though it had not paid my bills for the preceding nine months.

That department, naturally, refused to give an NOC because the phone was not theirs. So I traced out someone from my department of nine years ago and they gave the NOC. Now Airtel refused to honour a scanned copy received by email. So I got the original couriered, which they accepted but still did not change the phone's ownership on their records, at least till I last spoke to them, which was several weeks after submitting the NOC in the original.

Now Airtel wanted four photographs, which I gave. Their new objection was that these photographs were taken in a different year from the photograph on the passport. They were right, but had a government servant said so his 'bureaucratic' psychology would have been called into question.

After all their queries had been satisfied they still took a week or two to send me an SMS confirming that they had agreed to port my number. When they did they told me that the actual 'porting' would take place twelve days later, ie two days less than five months after my initial 'port' SMS to them. Till then I had to continue to pay expensive roaming charges.

On the appointed day I was on tour to Srinagar so, despite two hours of trying, the porting did not take place. This took three more days of calling them up. Now they wanted to know the number of my SIM card, which I had ripped open, as everyone does, in order to extricate the card. I was able to get the number from the shop where I had bought the card from.

At last, the new SIM started receiving signals – but not calls or messages.

I tried to call my brother but was directed to an Airtel number, which wanted me to confirm several facts about myself.

What was most bureaucratic was Airtel's insistence that my billing address would be the one mentioned on my passport, which was made several years ago and since when I had changed my address a few times. (I was told to go through another tedious process to get my address changed.) What followed was not just bureaucratic but downright idiotic.

My passport had been made when I was serving in the Raj Bhawan. Therefore, the Raj Bhawan was given as my address on the passport. Now Airtel's staffer wanted to know the name of some landmark near the Raj Bhawan before she would allow my number to be activated. I could not name any.

As anyone who knows India will tell you, every Raj Bhawan is itself a landmark, and almost all Raj Bhawans in India are very far from another landmark. In Raj Bhawan, Jammu's case just the drive from the main road is almost a kilometre; in Srinagar the drive from the nearest landmark (the Palace hotel) is almost three kilometres. What 'nearby landmark' will you mention if you are a jawan posted in the Rashtrapati Bhawan campus in Delhi? Or an employee of Calcutta's Victoria Memorial or Mumbai's International Airport or Chennai's LIC building? Will you mention the name of some nearby office, hotel, shop or tea stall? Which one, because there are so many of them?

Airtel's objections, queries and long delays can all be justified from some cautious point of view. However, if a government servant had done all this the psychology of the entire bureaucracy would have been called into question, abused and made fun of.

My number was finally 'ported' exactly five months after my first 'port' message to Airtel.

Case 4: Do MNC Employees have Better Psychologies?

Government-owned banks are, rightly, reviled for their primitive methods and service.

However, at least they do not go back on their word.

In the late 1980s Citibank expected a minimum balance of ₹ 10,000 in savings accounts, when government-owned banks wanted only ₹ 100. Citibank had a right to do so. It could even have insisted on a minimum balance of ₹ 1,000 crore if it wished: for all new accounts. In a span of two years Citibank raised the minimum limit to ₹ 1.5 lakh, and imposed this fifteen-fold (1,500%) increase on existing account holders. Many of these people had no option but to close their accounts, losing considerable amounts of money (and time), because they had conveyed their Citibank account number to companies in which they had shares and fixed deposits, so that their dividends could be deposited automatically in their Citibank account. Thanks to Citibank's new minimum limit, its account holders had to recall the names of all companies in which they had invested money, send them new advices and hope that they had not forgotten to inform any company and no dividend warrant had got lost during this transition.

Standard Chartered bank employees are notorious for repeatedly troubling (and embarrassing) account holders by not honouring their ECS (electronic clearance) mandates. Secondly, they expect account holders to set aside all other work and provide the bank the same documentation (PAN Card, proof of residence etc) once in every three years or so. If the account holder is too busy to do so, his account is frozen, even if he has been with the bank since its opening in India (or the acquisition of that branch). If the bank's courier cannot find the account holder's house, again his account gets frozen.

Standard Chartered's excuse is that the Finance Ministry's KYC (know your customer) norms oblige them to do so. However, government-owned banks like the State Bank of India do not make clients go through all this paperwork once they have opened an account with them.

There used to an MNC bank that was first called National Grindlays, then ANZ Grindlays and finally Standard Chartered Grindlays before it just disappeared. It used to pay the highest salaries in India, at least at the entry level. It would recruit managers only from posh, English-speaking families.

In 1977 the government allowed all banks to charge ₹3 for every cheque credited to an individual's account. Some government-owned banks assured account holders that they would charge nothing. When Grindlays gave the same assurance, in writing, I decided to continue receiving cheques in my Grindlays account. However, I noticed that despite its assurance Grindlays was deducting ₹3 from every ₹100 cheque that I used to receive. (₹100 then was equal to around ₹4,500 in 2016.) In effect, in my case Grindlays was deducting 3% of every cheque that I received at that account. This was a huge percentage anywhere in the world.

I went over to Grindlays to complain that they had gone back on their written assurance without informing us of the change. Their posh manager ducked the main question about not having informed account holders. He told me that I should not complain because I could afford to pay that 3%.

I cannot recall a single government bureaucrat with that kind of an insensitive psychology.

The ONLY comparable event in the post-1947 history of India's government bureaucracy is the retrospective tax on Vodafone, which shattered the Indian economy. Because Grindlays' managers had an identical psychology, the bank tossed from buyer to buyer before vanishing altogether.

Moral: Many, perhaps the majority of Indian bureaucrats, have a sick psychology. However, they are sick not because they are bureaucrats. They are like that because they are Indians of a certain type.

Do All Bureaucrats have the Same Psychology?

Anyone who asserts that all bureaucrats have the same (or a broadly similar) psychology needs help – psychiatric help.

Quite apart from the fact that all humans are different and have different psychologies, if you insist on grouping bureaucrats into a few broad psychological 'types', you should at least account for dissimilarities along the following lines:

(i) 'Class' of employment:

(a) Security: The higher a bureaucrat is on the four-fold 'class' ladder the more insecure he is. (This, again, is true of the private sector. Lower paid and unionised employees are as secure as government bureaucrats. Even within senior journalists, the high flying ones on contract are insecure; those getting lower paid 'wage board' salaries are not.)

(b) Levels of education, acculturation and pre-employment achievements vary totally from one 'class' to another; and, within Group A services, from one service to another. Therefore, too, it would be a brave man who can say that a peon has the same psychology as a clerk (peons tend to focus on results, clerks on processes), and a patwari (village-level revenue official) the same as an auditor. Will a Kendriya Vidyalaya topper who gets into an IIT and then into a Group A service have the same psychology as someone who gets into a junior cadre and who did not have similar accomplishments at school and college?

Moral: Do not generalise about the psychology of the bureaucracy.

(c) The Nature of the 'Service' (Cadre), too, Determines Psychology: Foreign service officers tend to be more pleasant and less obnoxious than their twins in services where officers deal more with files and less with humans. (I have specific examples in mind, which made me come to this conclusion.) Forest service officers tend to develop a more noble and other-worldly approach towards life, and auditors sharp minds that spot details in files that others do not. But then auditors are not concerned about deadlines or the need to complete projects within fixed time periods. Engineers and IRTS (railway traffic) officers tend to develop result-oriented mindsets. IRAS (railway accounts) do not face the same pressures.

(ii-a) Central and State Governments: The psychologies of bureaucrats are totally different depending on whether they are working for the Central Government or a State. Officers who alternate between the two change at least some attitudes when they make the transition. In the States bureaucrats have to live with each other throughout their working lives. This can be good and bad. Relationships among colleagues are stronger, but that too are office politics and rivalries. At the centre things might be more professionally done but officers feel less impelled to complete projects or keep the public happy and contented.

(ii-b) British India *vs* 'Indian India': Officers in States formerly ruled by Maharajas are forced by the environment to be far more accessible than those in formerly British-ruled States, where, on the other hand, systems and processes are much better developed.

(ii-c) The Ethos of Individual States: A study showed that the judiciary in Karnataka had the best rate of disposal of cases; undivided Andhra Pradesh and Tamil Nadu followed. Even in the IAS we consider these three better administered than most other States. The culture of the people of these States is more technocratic. An officer from Bihar or UP posted in these three States will show higher output than in his own State, whereas a Kannadiga or Telugu-/Tamil-speaker in Bihar will have a rate of disposal at best marginally higher than his counterparts of local origin.

In north India Madhya Pradesh, Himachal Pradesh and Rajasthan have traditionally been considered good places for officers to work in. The local people are disciplined (and these States have known political stability) and this influences most bureaucrats' psychology.

In Kerala in particular but also in West Bengal and Tripura the emphasis is on honesty and financial probity, but not on results, leave alone developing the economy of these States. Bureaucrats' minds change accordingly.

The relatively more alert corporate culture of Mumbai rubs off on the way government bureaucrats and public sector executives work and behave in that city.

In Kashmir the people expect results and are not bothered if procedures are not followed; indeed, they love swashbuckling officers who take risks, are not shackled by rules and traditions and deliver results. This moulds the thinking of non-local officers as well.

What Most Bureaucrats have in Common

Despite all these differences, all bureaucrats' minds are influenced by the few things that they do have in common, across States, departments and service cadres:

(i) Security of Tenure: Officers of the three All-India Services, especially the Indian administrative and police services (and the State administrative and police services) are the most insecure among government servants. They are worried about transfers (which can be extremely stressful) and loss of reputation. Doctors, teachers and engineers, too, get kicked around and shunted to the villages but have longer tenures than administrative and police officers.

However, the insecurity of bureaucrats is nothing compared to that of top managers in the private sector, where there is a constant and real threat of loss of the present level of earnings. This affects the psychology of both government and private sector bureaucrats: in opposite ways. A mild degree of insecurity compels individuals to achieve better results at the work-place. Government bureaucrats are more secure than in the private sector and, therefore, less likely to chase results.

University staff is the most secure because they cannot be transferred anywhere or denied career progression. As a result teachers do not feel the need to teach better or research better; the few who do so because they are made that way. At many universities teachers organise themselves into cliques. I have seen incredible levels of pettiness at the few universities I have first-hand knowledge of. I have seen Vice-Chancellors refuse new research projects (and cancel existing ones) because they couldn't be bothered to exert themselves. I have seen a VC order an inquiry into how one of his juniors became an advisor to the State Government, something the VC wanted for himself but did not have the required technical qualifications.

Though bureaucrats' careers are not as secure as in government-owned universities, they are secure enough to not to have to strive for excellence or high results.

(ii) Women: In the case of women employees, the psychology of government bureaucrats is much better than in at least one newspaper, one advertising firm and several BPO (outsourcing) companies that I know. Female bureaucrats, from stenographers to secretaries, do not have to make compromises to reach the top of their respective ladders. This is an offshoot of the somewhat higher security of tenure in the government.

(iii) A Feeling of Being Shackled: Industrialist Anil Ambani rightly said that Indian bureaucrats are afraid of taking decisions because of the three Cs: CAG, CVC and CBI. Actually there are several more checks as well, including house committees, a shrill media.... All these were created, equally rightly, to ensure that there was no corruption or arbitrariness. However, corruption flourishes merrily despite all these checks, which have only succeeded in making bureaucrats take no risks or dynamic measures. (If I was able to take risks it was because my Chief Minister and most Chief Secretaries in the State and ministers and Civil Service bosses in the Centre supported me to the hilt.)

(iv) No Incentive to Perform Well: My friends in Indian private sector giants say that things are somewhat similar in large, bureaucratic private sector organisations, though I can't get myself to believe them. I have this illusion that at least in the private sector good results are rewarded.

In the government those who play safe are rewarded. With those who achieve high results the record is mixed: their success is sometimes actually held against them by jealous people immediately senior and immediately junior to them, but often appreciated by the highest in the government – Prime Ministers and Ministers.

Amitabh Kant, IAS, worked wonders not only for Kerala Tourism but also spearheaded the highly successful Incredible India campaign. And yet he had to go through mental torture for almost one year, which was front-paged by most national newspapers, which backed him. But there is God's justice. The Prime Minister and Cabinet Secretary backed him and, instead, removed the minister who was torturing him. His reputation was recognised by the next government, which made him in-charge of the even more successful Make in India campaign.

At least one of my bureaucrat seniors could not digest the ITDC's reasonable financial performance during my tenure. He played office politics which led to a sharp deterioration of ITDC's work culture after I left. However, as I said, there is God's justice. A minister (Mr Subodh Kant Sahai), whom I had never met, leave alone working under him, heard of my reputation and handpicked me for the highest Civil Service job in the Tourism ministry, though I was the Secretary of another ministry by then.

However, by and large, the best jobs and incentives like foreign assignments do not necessarily go to those with the best measurable performance.

Engineers who made the ITDC the only government organisation in India to be singled out for praise (on the front pages of all national newspapers, when other departments were being criticised) by the Commonwealth Games Committee for the 2010 Games, were victimised by the same office politics, rather than being rewarded.

(v) Low Sense of Ownership: Very few government and public sector bureaucrats have a sense of ownership towards their department, ministry or State, though they work there throughout their careers. I have always wondered how private sector companies, in which senior managers spend only a few years before moving to other companies, instil a sense of ownership in their employees. (Pilot of a private airline, that I was flying in, started speaking on the aeroplane's public address system. When he came to "Thank you for flying with ...", he paused for a moment, as if he was trying not to mention his previous airline out of habit and was trying to recall his present airline's name.)

At least in one Indian IT giant, of which I have deep personal knowledge, things are much worse than in the government. Employees pass off the retention of existing clients as the acquisition of new business, and the company's rules allow this. Rules (even for the daily lunch in the canteen) are as rigid as in the government. Office politics is much worse than in the Government of India and slightly worse than in State Governments. Attitudes towards allotting office space, equipment and teams are as cussed as in the government.

I am associated with a school for well to do children. The principal had no idea of the number by which the annual intake of students had declined during the three preceding years of his tenure. Naturally, therefore, he had done nothing to check the decline. His attitude was that the school belonged to its owners and not to him.

REFERENCES

1. I got the chargesheet withdrawn. Those two managers, who had reputations for integrity and hard work, paid me back with a 1,200%

increase in the profits of their division and an almost 12,000% increase in their turnover. Their careers, which could have been marred by that chargesheet, too, zoomed upwards after that.

2. I got this VP overruled by his bosses, whom I knew well. They, too, were amazed by his negativity, which was denying his company free, international publicity.

Epilogue

The judgment by the Nuremberg Trial Tribunal established after the Second World War that the subordinates should not obey the illegal orders of the superior. This created upheaval in the sea of tranquillity of bureaucracy. For the first time, the judgment questioned the unchallenged authority of bureaucrats to take shelter under the garb of orders of the superior in his organization.

Gradually, bureaucrats also collaborated with the political executives or masters for their unwarranted personal gains. Thirdly, the private sector became so powerful that it has surpassed the public sector run by the bureaucrats in terms of its dimensions and delivery of public benefits by it. Even then, bureaucrats continue to wield enormous regulatory as well as economic powers. Therefore, they are very egoistic. Their decision making impacts the life of general public. It is essential to study his psychology which is made of *inter alia* of his values, macro environment and the organization he is working in. It may differ from age to age and from country to country but the basic traits of a bureaucrat are universal as he is disciple of Weber.

Bureaucracy is a necessary evil. Even United Nations and its agencies are run by strong and robust bureaucracy. Even the behavioural aspects of bureaucrats differ from State to State in India.

Some bureaucrats are work-oriented, the other are feudal and aristocratic whereas the third category of bureaucrats are dull and rule-bound. Their only motto is to observe rules and regulations irrespective of their effect on people. Their goal is to protect their security of job. Therefore, it is now accepted solution that the steel frame security of bureaucrats should be loosened a little but it should not be 'hire and fire' maxim because it is bureaucracy which is permanent in government. The political executives come and go. And for broader public welfare and safety, a permanent Civil Service such as bureaucracy is a preferred option.

As bureaucracy is a stable organization, efforts should always be made to motivate its members through their psyche so that there is better delivery of public service and people get proper justice and due share in development undertaken by the government. After the bureaucrats are motivated initially or at any later stage of their career, it should be ensured that they remain motivated, so that overall objectives of the polity are achieved.

It is a fact that the working as bureaucrat is not in a straight line. He has to work among conflicting claims, and counter claims and has to take decision on his own at his position. He has also to please his boss, along with meeting demands of his family, peers and friends. As a result, he develops mental tension and his outward calm personality is in fact a ocean of disturbances. The system has to take care of him so that he can deliver better output and requisite results.

All governments in the world are conscious of the vital role played by bureaucrats in running them and to reach their largesse to public at large. It is equally important that bureaucrats should also realize that they are not inevitable. They should maintain their mental balances. They are not inevitable but should make themselves indispensable by serving people or their clients or stake-holders with personal integrity, efficiency and sincerity of purpose. Then only the bureaucrats will achieve their past glory and will be adored and respected by people as in the past.

Index